A *Woman's Guide* to
SPIRITUAL WARFARE

REVISED AND UPDATED EDITION

A *Woman's Guide* to
SPIRITUAL WARFARE

HOW TO PROTECT YOUR HOME, FAMILY AND FRIENDS FROM SPIRITUAL DARKNESS

QUIN SHERRER AND RUTHANNE GARLOCK

Chosen

a division of Baker Publishing Group
Minneapolis, Minnesota

Published by Chosen Books
11400 Hampshire Avenue South
Bloomington, Minnesota 55438
www.chosenbooks.com

Chosen Books is a division of
Baker Publishing Group, Grand Rapids, Michigan

Previously published by Servant Publications and Regal Books

Printed in the United States of America

Library of Congress Cataloging-in-Publication Data
Names: Sherrer, Quin, author. | Garlock, Ruthanne, author.
Title: A woman's guide to spiritual warfare : how to protect your home, family and friends
    from spiritual darkness / Quin Sherrer and Ruthanne Garlock.
Description: Revised and Updated Edition. | Minneapolis, Minnesota : Chosen, 2017. |
    Includes bibliographical references.
Identifiers: LCCN 2016034861 | ISBN 9780800797997 (trade paper : alk. paper)
Subjects: LCSH: Women—Religious life. | Spiritual warfare.
Classification: LCC BV4527 .S43 2017 | DDC 248.8/43—dc23
LC record available at https://lccn.loc.gov/2016034861

Cover design by Rob Williams, InsideOutCreativeArts

17 18 19 20 21 22 23   7 6

Contents

Acknowledgments

Thanks to all those who prayed for us while this project and its revision were under way.

Thanks also to the women who allowed us to share their stories—defeats as well as victories. Your transparency enriches this book and will encourage our readers.

Also we wish to acknowledge and thank three special women for their editorial support for this book's publishing success: Ann Spangler, who cast the vision for the original edition; and Kim Bangs and Jane Campbell, who have guided the work for the revised editions.

Special love and gratitude to the Lord Jesus Christ, our commander in chief, who calls us, equips us and leads us into battle.

And to the Holy Spirit, our teacher and faithful guide.

Introduction

Soon after the first edition of this title was released in 1991, it hit the top-selling list for Christian books in the spiritual warfare category. In fact, it kept that rating for six years, and both men and women were reading it as a classic on the topic. I (Quin) admit it was not a subject I was eager to write about when Servant senior editor Ann Spangler first proposed the idea, but we agreed to take on the project.

Ruthanne and I interviewed dozens of women who had successfully found victory, and they readily shared their scriptural strategies and insights. It was a great learning experience for us, plus we also gained great appreciation for our many prayer partners who faithfully prayed during the process.

Once, I (Quin) was on a flight from Orlando to Atlanta and introduced myself to the woman sitting beside me. As soon as I mentioned my name, she cried out, "You wrote that book that helped save my marriage and my children—*A Woman's Guide to Spiritual Warfare*! I copied the prayers in it and asked my husband to pray them aloud with me every day. Our daughter was falling into bad company, but we used those prayers and examples to give us hope. Today we are a family following the Lord and active in a church."

A while back, a friend called me from Virginia. "Just wanted you to know I minister in a prison here," she said. "A woman I was talking to about the Lord was reading your book—behind bars yet!—and said it was really helping her."

I (Ruthanne) have had countless similar encounters with women who have told me that reading the book and praying the prayers in it saved their marriages, healed broken relationships with prodigal children or helped them break free from bondage. A woman in Lima, Peru, read the Spanish edition and wrote, "*A Woman's Guide to Spiritual Warfare* is helping me to keep going after my mother's death. I have been attacked by the enemy, until I read your book and started to rebuke him."

One friend used to come to my resource table every summer at an annual ministry gathering and buy several copies to give to the military wives she was mentoring. Some have told me they keep the book on their bedside table so they can refer to it often. Readers tell us they not only keep their own copy handy, but also buy additional ones to give away. Several times women have come to my table to buy the book, saying, "I had my own copy but loaned it out and never got it back. I have to have another one!"

Although we do not claim to be experts on the subject, we have gained a lot of knowledge about spiritual warfare through our research and study, and especially through our own times "in the trenches." This revision is an accumulation of our combined experience, plus many testimonies from women just like you who are learning to be skilled warriors.

Today's women face unique difficulties that need to be addressed in the context of spiritual warfare: single parenting, troubled marriages, demanding careers, the "supermom" syndrome, media influence, abortion, coping with addicted children and spouses, financial pressures—the list goes on and on.

Through this practical handbook, we aim to help women understand the *why* and the *how* of spiritual warfare based on biblical examples and contemporary experiences. In these pages, we will address such questions as:

- What is spiritual warfare?
- Who is the enemy, and who started the war?
- Is every mishap from Satan?
- What weapons are we to use?
- If Jesus won the victory, why do we have to fight?
- What about the battle in the mind?
- How can we distinguish between God's voice and the enemy's voice?
- How do we become vulnerable to Satan's work?
- How can we feel secure against spiritual attacks?
- How do we avoid becoming battle weary?

As we address these and other questions, providing experiences to illustrate them, you will gain insight and confidence about fighting your own spiritual battles. You will also be equipped to encourage and strengthen others who may be under attack. Of course, Jesus has done everything necessary to ensure our victory over Satan. But as we are faithful to the call to spiritual combat, we reenforce what Christ did at Calvary.

Whether you are a seasoned intercessor or a new volunteer, this book is for you. It will bring encouragement, hope and equipping, and it will give you new Scripture ammunition for your prayer arsenal (see Appendix 1 for even more).

We invite you to turn the page and embark upon your new prayer journey!

Quin Sherrer and Ruthanne Garlock

1

But I Never Wanted to Be in a Battle!

> For our struggle is not against flesh and blood, but against the rulers, against the authorities, against the powers of this dark world and against the spiritual forces of evil in the heavenly realms.
>
> Ephesians 6:12

"I resist you in the name of Jesus and command you to go!" Claudia said with a quavering voice. To her amazement, the hideous black leopard turned and ran. Startled, she awoke from the bad dream and sat up in bed.

"I realized the Lord was teaching me in my dream to do spiritual warfare—that the name of Jesus really has power," shared this trim brunette. "I had accepted Jesus as my Savior and Lord and had received the Holy Spirit. But then my mind was bombarded with fear and condemnation. I loved God more than anything, yet the enemy made me think I had blasphemed the Holy Spirit and would never be able to please God."

Claudia had never received any teaching on how to deal with fear. She had heard some comments about spiritual warfare but had no clue what that meant. She thought she simply had to endure this struggle in exchange for her salvation. Then came her dream.

"In the dream, I was constantly being pursued by a huge black leopard," she said. "I pushed it out the door and it came in the window. Everywhere I went, it followed me. I was terrified. Then I sensed the Lord say to me, *Claudia, resist the leopard in the name of Jesus.* In my dream I stopped running, turned and faced the leopard, and commanded it to leave in Jesus' name. I was happily surprised to see it flee!"

Claudia's friend Jean took her to a woman who ministers in deliverance because there was witchcraft in Claudia's family background and because she had used drugs in college. The Lord broke these and many related bondages.

Jean became Claudia's prayer partner and began training her in scriptural truths. "Now," Claudia said, "I know a Christian can truly be victorious over the spiritual forces of evil that Paul talks about in Ephesians."

Is the Devil Real?

My (Quin's) subject was prayer. My audience: three dozen pastors' wives. I had been asked to teach a weekend workshop at a rustic lodge hidden away in the Georgia pines. But after the first session, during which I had briefly discussed spiritual warfare, the leader who had invited me knocked on my door.

"Quin, you've offended some of our women here," she said apologetically. "Several of them have Ph.D.s, and they don't believe Christians need to fight the devil in our day and age. Please tone down your message."

I had shared some basic guidelines on intercession and how to pray the Word of God as a means of opposing the enemy. Then I had explained that Satan—not another person—is our enemy and that we need to be on guard against his tactics. I was stunned to think a group of pastors' wives would find such teaching offensive. But I agreed to adapt my material.

The apostle Paul's many references to spiritual warfare clearly indicate that he considered battling against the powers of darkness to be normal activity for Christians. But my experience at the retreat offers a graphic example of a common attitude among many Christians today.

"Spiritual warfare? Those two words don't go together!" one friend exclaimed upon hearing of plans for this book.

We might ask these people, "Don't you even believe the devil exists?" Well, yes, they do—theologically speaking. But the tendency is to think of Satan not as a personality or a being who affects us directly but as simply a pervasive influence of evil in the world.

In fact, a Barna Group survey states that four out of ten Christians (40 percent) strongly agreed that Satan "is not a living being but is a symbol of evil," while only about 30 percent of Christians indicated they believe Satan is real. Some were honest enough to say they were not sure what they believe about the existence of Satan. Regarding the survey, George Barna said:

> Most Americans, even those who say they are Christian, have doubts about the intrusion of the supernatural into the natural world. Hollywood has made evil accessible and tame, making Satan and demons less worrisome than the Bible suggests they really are. It's hard for achievement-driven, self-reliant, independent people to believe that their lives can be impacted by unseen forces.[1]

C. S. Lewis wisely wrote, "There are two equal and opposite errors into which our race can fall about the devils. One is to disbelieve in their existence. The other is to believe, and to feel an excessive and unhealthy interest in them."[2]

Some of the pastors' wives at that retreat had apparently fallen into the first error. Either they did not believe in Satan's existence, or they mistakenly felt there was nothing they should be doing about it.

"Maybe the next time one of these women faces a direct attack from the enemy in her life, she'll think about what I said," I told my prayer partner who had accompanied me to the retreat. "Well, you gave them the Word of God," my friend assured me. "And His Word never returns void."

The next afternoon, as we were packing my car to leave, a young pastor's wife ran up to me. "I just want you to know that your first lesson really opened my eyes," she said with exuberance. "I'm going home to apply some of those spiritual warfare methods, and I know things are going to change! I now realize my rebellious teenage son is not the enemy. I intend to use Scripture as a weapon to fight the devil, just as you showed us."

How Does He Attack Us?

The biblical Deborah, a prophetess and judge in Israel whose story is told in the fourth chapter of Judges, challenges us to lay aside some of our own worthy interests and activities to deal with the spiritual battles at hand. Deborah held court under a palm tree between Bethel and Ramah at a time when Israel was suffering bitter oppression under Jabin, a Canaanite king who had defeated Israel and occupied its land.

The name Jabin means "cunning," and the Canaanite word comes from a root word meaning "to humiliate or bring under subjection." Deborah must have heard daily reports of Jabin's cruel treatment. His army general, Sisera, terrorized the people with his nine hundred chariots of iron, while Israel's army had almost no weapons for its defense. No doubt Deborah became increasingly incensed over the situation and joined the people of Israel in crying out to the Lord for deliverance.

We modern Deborahs need to feel that same indignation about Satan's work. By engaging in prayer and spiritual warfare, we can take a stand against the enemy's oppression in our own world.

The enemy works in many ways today—some more subtle than others. It seems his iron chariots come in all sizes! Perhaps you recognize yourself in one or more of these everyday attacks (which a friend of ours calls *household sins*):

- Strife and disharmony disrupting family relationships
- A defensive response to a loved one being unjustly treated by another Christian, resulting in increasing bitterness and cynicism
- Anger erupting at the slightest provocation
- Guilt over one's seeming lack of success as a Christian
- Envy when comparing one's own circumstances with friends' seemingly carefree lives
- Frequent insecurity and anxiety about the future
- An inconsistent prayer life and prayers that seem to bounce back in one's face

A friend once said to me, "Quin, I never wanted to have to fight the devil. I just wanted to remain a normal Christian, go to church, mind my own business and not cause trouble." But when her son got into drugs, she learned spiritual warfare out of necessity.

Thousands of women feel they have just been tending to business as usual, trying their best to live a good Christian life. Suddenly an iron chariot comes roaring through their household, church, business or community, thrusting them into confrontation with the enemy—and they cry out, "Help!"

You may be facing one of these battles, too, which many other women have shared with us:

- Your pregnant, unwed daughter is convinced that getting an abortion is the answer to her dilemma.
- You learn your child is on drugs, and the dealer has been attending the church youth group.
- You discover a cache of pornographic literature in your husband's closet.
- A teenage acquaintance confides that she was sexually abused by her father, who is a deacon in the church.
- An adult porn shop opens in your neighborhood, and local authorities seem indifferent to the situation.
- Your teenager goes into rebellion, gets caught up in rock music and runs away from home to join a satanist group.
- A widow whom you and your husband befriended convinces him it is God's will for him to divorce you and marry her.

Such situations confront many Christian women today—women whose eyes are opening to the spiritual battle already happening around them, even though they feel unprepared to fight. No longer do they need to be persuaded that a war is on. They are looking for guidance as to how to engage the battle.

What Can Deborah Teach Us?

We can learn much from Deborah about how to deal with spiritual enemies. After suffering twenty long years under Jabin's oppression, the people of Israel began to beseech God for deliverance. He responded by instructing Deborah to say to Barak, the general of Israel's army:

> "The LORD, the God of Israel, commands you: 'Go, take with you ten thousand men of Naphtali and Zebulun and lead the way to Mount Tabor. I will lead Sisera, the commander of Jabin's army, with his chariots and his troops to the Kishon River and give him into your hands.'"
>
> Judges 4:6–7

Barak, who had faced this formidable enemy before, was fearful—and with good cause. A weak volunteer army with no chariots and few weapons was no match for Sisera's well-trained army of a hundred thousand men![3] But Barak was assessing the situation strictly from a logistics point of view. Facts and truth are not always the same. The truth was that God had promised victory in spite of the odds if Israel would obey Him. Deborah— who was called "a mother in Israel" (Judges 5:7)—was willing to stake the nation's future on that promise. What courage it took to give such bold instructions to Israel's army general! But she acted on God's truth, not on the circumstantial fact that the Israelites were outnumbered by their enemy.

Barak agreed to go, but only if Deborah went with him. After all, she was the one with the word from God. So in order to see her people liberated, Deborah assumed the role of a military commander to accompany Barak in leading the troops to battle (see Judges 4:8–10). It was a necessary but unpleasant task.

Deborah received specific orders from God about where Israel's troops were to be placed: Mount Tabor. As they approached the Kishon River, Sisera received intelligence reports as to Israel's movements. He gathered his army and went out against Israel, unaware that he was cooperating with God's plan.

This was the greatest display of Sisera's military might Barak and Deborah had ever seen. He had mobilized all his soldiers, weapons and chariots to annihilate Israel's weak army. Barak, surveying the situation from his vantage point on the mountain, may have had second thoughts about going into battle against Sisera. But Deborah was not deterred by this show of strength. She knew it was Sisera's *last* show!

As Sisera's army came close to the Kishon River, Scripture suggests that God caused a freak rainstorm, which blinded the soldiers and caused the river to flood, sweeping the iron chariots downstream (see Judges 5:4, 20–22). The name Kishon is from a root word meaning "to ensnare." Scripture records the outcome:

> Then Deborah said to Barak, "Go! This is the day the LORD has given Sisera into your hands. Has not the LORD gone ahead of you?" So Barak went down Mount Tabor, with ten thousand men following him. At Barak's advance, the LORD routed Sisera and all his chariots and army by the sword, and Sisera got down from his chariot and fled on foot.
>
> . . . All Sisera's troops fell by the sword; not a man was left.
>
> Judges 4:14–16

One version of the text says, "Then the Lord threw the enemy into a panic. . . . Not one man was left alive" (verses 15–16 TLB).

Sisera took refuge in the tent of Jael, a Canaanite woman whom he thought he could trust. But Jael, choosing to align herself with the people of God, was not content to be a passive bystander in this war. Using household tools at hand—a mallet and a tent stake—she killed the enemy commander. End of Sisera. End of those dreaded iron chariots.

Amazing, isn't it? Two women were the key players in this drama in which God enabled a weak army, outnumbered ten to one, to win a resounding victory. Seven penetrating words end the story: "Then the land had peace forty years" (Judges 5:31).

Deborah and Barak were assured of victory because they battled according to God's instructions. God would not do it for them without their effort, nor did He reveal the entire strategy in advance. They had to obey God without knowing all the reasons why. God determined the place of the battle and told them how many soldiers to take.

When Deborah and Barak obeyed, doing what was possible for them to do, God responded by doing the impossible, which only He could do. Deborah applied seven keys to ensure victory in the assault against the enemy's iron chariots:

1. She recognized that it was a *spiritual* battle and that God was going ahead of her small army.
2. She obeyed God's instructions, trusting His strategy.
3. She did not focus on the seeming strength of the enemy.
4. She did not waver in her confidence in God's Word.
5. She refused to be deterred by her colleague's lack of spiritual vision.
6. She never compromised with the enemy.
7. She gave praise and glory to God for the victory.

These same principles apply in the spiritual battles we face. We, too, can use these seven keys to see our enemy defeated. Final success is assured, but we have to seek God's direction and put forth some effort in obedience.

Do You Believe in This?

I (Quin) remember back in 1972 when an iron chariot rolled through the church my mom was attending in Destin, Florida.[4] While visiting her there, I reluctantly agreed to attend one of the church's small home prayer meetings on a Friday night. I soon learned the group had gathered to pray for Bill, a 31-year-old Air Force officer who attended their church. He was dying of acute leukemia at a hospital in Mississippi.

The prayer leader told me the doctors had diagnosed Bill with the worst form of leukemia, with his bone marrow mass-producing cancerous blood cells too rapidly for chemotherapy to be effective. The medical experts believed Bill had reached the end of his fight, and they did not expect him to live through the weekend.

The group began crying out for God to intervene, but such intense prayer was completely foreign to me in those days. Not knowing how to participate, I told the Lord to count me out. I did not know whether He still healed or not, but if He did, I asked Him to hear the prayers of those gathered in the home, as they were praying with great faith and boldness.

One man shocked me when he began shouting, "Satan, we give you notice that you and your demonic forces cannot have Bill Lance. He is God's property, and we are standing in the gap for his complete healing. Spirits of infirmity, leave him, in Jesus' name." It was my first exposure to spiritual warfare.

These people really believe that Bill is going to be healed, I thought to myself. They told me that a few weeks earlier, the church had held a special healing service for him. As Bill knelt at the altar, Pastor Forrest Mobley and a group of elders had laid hands on him and had prayed that he would be healed. Here I was, a Christian at a home prayer meeting, unsure about the whole concept of healing for today, just looking on as this group battled for a man's life.

Later that same night, in the military hospital where he was being treated, Bill and his wife, Sharon, repeated the Lord's Prayer together in his room, as they always did each night. Suddenly Bill began to sob. He later reported that he felt fire, like a charge of light, shooting through his body. Somehow he knew the presence of Jesus had filled the room.

The next morning, when doctors examined a bone marrow sample from his chest, there were no signs of cancerous cells. In fact, the sample was normal. Bill believed the hot light he had felt penetrating his body the night before had been God's healing touch flooding through him. You can imagine the joy those intercessors felt when they received the good report.

I have kept in touch with Bill over the years since then and am glad to report he is still well and very active. He told me on the phone a while back, "My career allows me to follow my passion and live a blessed life, as Sharon and I participate in church activities and our children and grandchildren live nearby."

As for me, I no longer doubt that Jesus is our healer. In fact, a year after Bill's healing, I wrote down his testimony and won a prestigious writing award, which launched me on my writing career and my understanding of spiritual warfare.

Do you believe this war is really happening? And do you believe women have a part to play? Our answer is an unequivocal yes—a woman's place is in this war! We believe women have a special interest in this battle. After all, our involvement in the war began with the woman and the serpent in the Garden of Eden. And it is the seed of the woman—Jesus—who has bruised the head of the serpent and secured the enemy's defeat.

We recognize, as Deborah did, that God has gone ahead of us to defeat the enemy, but He wants us involved in the battle. And as Claudia learned from experience, we have authority in the name of Jesus.

Now let's take a closer look at our enemy.

Prayer

Thank You, Lord, for showing me that Satan is an enemy who seeks to steal, kill and destroy Your purposes in my life. Help me to learn from Deborah's example that as I put my trust in You, I will receive strength and wisdom to fight my battles. I praise You in advance for victories that will bring honor and glory to Your name. Amen.

2

Who Is the Enemy, and What Does He Want from Me?

So the Lᴏʀᴅ God said to the serpent, ". . . I will put enmity between you and the woman, and between your offspring and hers; he will crush your head, and you will strike his heel."

Genesis 3:14–15

Satan is our archenemy. Scripture clearly confirms that he is the foe of every human being, starting with Adam and Eve. The name Satan actually means "adversary, or one who opposes." Yet as we discussed in the previous chapter, any mention of warfare with this enemy tends to repel many believers.

"Satan, demons, evil principalities and powers—these are scary things that frighten people," some Christians say. "It's just too spooky!"

But to ignore this enemy and hope he will ignore us is both unrealistic and hazardous. Missionary Arthur Mathews wrote:

The terrifying fact of a hostile world of evil and malicious spirits paralyzes many Christians into inactivity and unwillingness to seek out biblical answers and to apply them. . . . There are many clear indications of Satan's motives and methods given us in the Bible, if only we would heed them. . . . His central purpose is to pull God from His throne in the minds of men and to take that throne himself.[1]

To be effective in spiritual warfare, we need to be aware of the enemy's motives and tactics as revealed in Scripture. We need also to give attention to the many more references that assure victory to the persevering prayer warrior.

Why Satan Hates You and Me

Ever since God created Adam and Eve and placed them in the Garden of Eden, Satan has had a special hostility toward women. This fallen archangel, fuming with anger toward God and His creatures, lurked about the Garden, looking for a place where he could get a foothold and break the loving relationship between God and human beings.

Pride and rebellion led to Satan's own fall from heaven. Ultimately, he induced Eve to succumb to those same sins. The serpent and the daughters of Eve have been at enmity ever since. Satan not only hated Eve, but he also hates all her offspring—including you and me and those we love and want to protect.

This hatred toward Eve's offspring was expressed centuries ago by the sacrifice of children to evil gods. Then at Jesus' birth, through King Herod's order to kill all the babies under age two, Satan tried to murder the Messiah. He failed. Later he engineered Jesus' crucifixion and thought he had won at last. Actually, that was Satan's biggest mistake. Jesus' sacrificial death, burial and resurrection fulfilled the Father's plan to atone for sin and nullify Satan's plan. Scripture declares, "The reason the Son of God appeared was to destroy the devil's work" (1 John 3:8).

Godly women remain a frustration to Satan. Think about it—women bring human beings into the world, and Satan hates humans. He still tries to do away with them through child sacrifice, abortion and sexual trafficking.

Jesus completed the work the Father gave Him to do on earth, and the enemy can do nothing to change that perfect plan of salvation. But Satan *does* keep people from hearing the message; he also distorts and misrepresents the message. In other words, he vents his rage against the Father by taking vengeance on us. Satan tries to prevent our deliverance and tries to keep us alienated from God, knowing this frustrates God's desire to see us reconciled to Himself.

Paul explains it:

> If our gospel is veiled, it is veiled to those who are perishing. The god of this age has blinded the minds of unbelievers, so that they cannot see the light of the gospel that displays the glory of Christ, who is the image of God.
>
> 2 Corinthians 4:3–4

We then must oppose the spirits of darkness that blind and deceive the minds of the hearers. We must also resist evil forces trying to hinder our reaching people with the good news of salvation and freedom. Our goal is to see men and women—believers and unbelievers—set free from the bondage of Satan by the power of the blood of Jesus.

Bible teacher Dean Sherman makes the point that God and Satan are not equally powerful forces standing in opposition to each other. Satan is merely a created being, while God is "the great uncreated Creator."[2] Speaking of Satan's attempt to exalt himself and become like God, Sherman says:

What Satan did was absolutely ludicrous. Yet we, as finite, puny beings . . . think we can run our own lives without God. To try to live without God is to try to be God. This is exactly the absurd and insane pride that entered Satan's heart, and sadly, we all have it. . . . The being called Satan is merely a fallen archangel who received his name because he opposed God. He is also our adversary. We must consider him to be that—no more and no less.[3]

Though this enemy opposes us—though he hates us and does all he can to thwart God's plans for our redemption and freedom—his strategies are doomed to failure when faced with the power of God. God intends for us to use that power to oppose our enemy. He intends for us to use the authority that Jesus provides to believers (see Luke 10:19–20).

How the Enemy Works

We find in Scripture many names attributed to Satan and many descriptions of him that reveal both his methods and his character:

- "crafty" (Genesis 3:1)
- the deceiving "serpent" (Genesis 3:13)
- "the foe and the avenger" (Psalm 8:2)
- "the destroyer" (Isaiah 54:16)
- "the tempter" (Matthew 4:3; 1 Thessalonians 3:5)
- "the evil one" (Matthew 6:13; John 17:15)
- "the ruler of the demons [Beelzebub]" (Matthew 12:24 NKJV)
- "a murderer" (John 8:44)
- "a liar and the father of lies" (John 8:44)
- "the god of this age" (2 Corinthians 4:4)
- "an angel of light" (2 Corinthians 11:14)
- "the ruler of the kingdom of the air" (Ephesians 2:2)

- "the dragon" (Revelation 12:7)
- "that ancient serpent" (Revelation 12:9)
- "the accuser" (Revelation 12:10)

Journalist and author McCandlish Phillips deftly describes the way Satan operates:

> Consider the tactics of an enemy in battle. The enemy finds it far easier to send death upon his target if he conceals and hides his own position, so that he may strike by sudden surprise. . . . To obtain this advantage, the enemy moves in darkness, by stealth, and takes his position of advantage over the target in a hidden or camouflaged place. . . . The less the intended victims know of his existence, his position, his intention, and his power, the greater the advantage to him in bringing injury or death upon them.
>
> These are the tactics of Satan toward man. The less you know about Satan, the better he likes it. Your ignorance of his tactics confers an advantage upon him, but he prefers that you do not even credit his existence. If you do not believe that he is, then you will do nothing to prepare yourself, or your family, or your children, against his activities, and by that neglect many are made his victims.[4]

In other words, Satan moves in stealth by turning our attention toward the wrong target.

Many years ago, I (Ruthanne) came upon a striking picture of this. I was accompanying my late husband, John, on a ministry trip to Guatemala. One day our host took us to the ancient city of Antigua to visit a historical museum. This region had once been inhabited by the Mayan Indians, but the Spanish conquered the area in the early 1500s. A huge mural in the museum depicts the conflict.

The Mayan Indians—who fought with bow and arrow—were known to be brave, fierce warriors. But the Spanish soldiers had a distinct advantage because they wore armor, and they had horses and guns. Horses were unknown in the Western hemisphere at that time. So when the Indians saw one of these swift-footed animals with an armored soldier attached, they thought it was all one creature. They aimed at the horse, not realizing that the real enemy was the soldier astride the horse. Their arrows felled the horses in great numbers, but the armored soldiers jumped from their mounts and shot the Indians with their muskets.

The Mayans were massacred by the hundreds, and the Spanish seized control of the entire region.

"What a great illustration for spiritual warfare!" I exclaimed to John as we looked at the wall-to-wall painting. "The Indians were defeated because they failed to recognize the real enemy riding on the horse's back—and that's exactly what happens to countless Christians. They shoot at one another instead of fighting the devil."

"Well, then," John responded, "when another person confronts us with meanness and malice, we'd better remind ourselves, 'He's not the enemy; he's only the horse!'" Perhaps a laughable analogy, but graphic nonetheless.

In many instances, Satan does his work unhindered simply because Christians are apathetic or too preoccupied to take notice. Edith Schaeffer says:

> There is a deafness, blindness, insensitivity of touch and feeling among many Christians who refuse to recognize the war in which *they* are involved, and who are spiritually "playing a violin" while the enemy attacks and scores victories unchallenged, given no resistance. . . . We are as stupid and negligent as any of the "Neros" who ever lived, if we simply entertain ourselves with Christian diversions and let ourselves and our children be attacked and devoured without entering into the army and setting up the defense we have been instructed to prepare.[5]

The stakes are too high for us to let Satan move in our lives unhindered. We must be informed and equipped to fight in this war.

Why We Must Fight

We can compare our experiences in spiritual warfare with those of the children of Israel when God told them to go in and possess Canaan. They found heathen tribes in the Promised Land. God instructed them to drive out the tribes, and He promised to help them win their battles as long as they obeyed Him (see Joshua 23:6–13).

But, sad to say, Israel did not obey God. The Israelites compromised with their enemies, intermarried with the Canaanite tribes and took up idol worship and other heathen practices. The tribes they should have driven out became snares for them, and they never fully possessed their Promised Land. In the end they were taken into captivity.

Just as Israel had to fight enemy tribes to possess the land, so Christians today must fight. The difference is, Israel fought flesh-and-blood enemies, while our struggle is against principalities and powers of the unseen world (see Ephesians 6:12).

Many Christians hold the notion that once they are believers, covered by the blood of Jesus, they are immune to the enemy's influence. True, Jesus' blood cleanses us from all sin. And because we belong to Him, we have authority over all the power of the enemy (see Luke 10:19; Ephesians 1:22). But we still have the freedom of choice. At any time, we can choose *not* to obey God and *not* to avail ourselves of the power of the blood of Jesus. That wrong choice makes us vulnerable to the enemy.

Another factor to consider is that we are members of a fallen race. Our basic human weaknesses make us susceptible to the enemy's activity. Though God's great power far exceeds the power of Satan, we humans are no match for the devil if we are operating in our own strength.

More than three hundred years ago, Puritan pastor William Gurnall wrote this advice:

If you are going to take shelter under this attribute [God's almighty power], you must stay within its shade. What good will the shadow of a mighty rock do if we sit in the open sun? That is to say, if we wander away from God's protection by venturing into the heat of temptation, we should not be surprised when our faith grows faint and we stumble and fall into sin. We are weak in ourselves; our strength lies in the rock of God's almightiness. It should be our constant habitation.[6]

It is important to avoid these two extremes: first, blaming the devil for everything that goes wrong, when it could be a result of our own weaknesses or poor choices; second, not recognizing when Satan and his cohorts are at work against us or our loved ones, and failing to take authority over them.

To the degree we choose to walk in our own selfish ways instead of submitting to God's plan and purpose, we allow the enemy to gain a foothold in our lives. Thus Scripture admonishes us, "'In your anger do not sin' . . . do not give the devil a foothold" (Ephesians 4:26, 27). And again, "Be alert and of sober mind. Your enemy the devil prowls around like a roaring lion looking for someone to devour. Resist him, standing firm in the faith" (1 Peter 5:8–9).

Paul shares his experiences of spiritual warfare: "I have fought the good fight, I have finished the race, I have kept the faith. . . . Demas, because he loved this world, has deserted me" (2 Timothy 4:7, 10).

The enemy's attempt to draw us into sin causes our inner conflict. But if we choose to obey God, He gives us success in these skirmishes. Then we are empowered to battle outwardly, dispelling the powers of darkness and setting other captives free. The apostle Paul said he disciplined his body so that sins of his flesh would not cause him to lose that inner battle and be disqualified from doing the Lord's work (see 1 Corinthians 9:26–27).

We see tragic consequences today in the lives of those who fail to follow Paul's counsel:

- A Bible-school graduate goes back to her old group of friends, and soon she is hooked on drugs again.
- A former missionary leaves his wife and children to become a leader in a New Age group.
- A prominent preacher sternly condemns sin (while winning many converts to the Lord) and then confesses to being addicted to pornography.
- A lawyer with a twenty-year record as an excellent Christian businessman is caught embezzling $200,000 from the local school board.

Despite these people's exploits for God, they lost the inner contest by walking out from under the sheltering rock of God's almighty power. Of course the Father's mercy allows for them to be restored and healed. But how much better "to be made new in the attitude of your minds" (Ephesians 4:23) and to walk in mastery over these temptations and struggles!

God has provided all we need to defeat this adversary of ours—both the enemy within and the enemy without. We have "the full armor of God" (Ephesians 6:11) and weapons with "divine power to demolish strongholds" (2 Corinthians 10:4).

How We Can Oppose Him

Sue, a former student, provides a great example of the importance of seeing the enemy for who he is and using one's authority to defeat him. She called one day and asked me (Ruthanne) to pray for her unsaved father, who had terminal cancer. Sue and her mother had prayed for years for him to accept Jesus. Now near death, he was very bitter, blaming God for his illness.

"How can we lead him to Christ when he is so angry?" Sue asked me.

"The problem is, he's believing Satan's lie that God is his enemy," I responded. "He needs to see that God is his only source of help. I suggest you bind the lying spirit that has deceived him. Then just shower your father with unconditional love; don't preach to him anymore."

Sue's mother and brother picked up extension phones, and I prayed while they agreed, saying, "Thank You, Father, that it is Your desire to bring Sue's dad into Your Kingdom. We take authority in the name of Jesus and bind the deceiving spirits that are lying to him. We ask the Holy Spirit to reveal the truth that You love him. Lord, cause him to come to his senses and escape from the trap of the devil. We ask this in Jesus' name, Amen."

I suggested they continue this strategy. "Use the authority Jesus gave you to forbid the enemy to speak to your father," I said.

About six weeks later, Sue called to tell me her father had died. But just before he died, he received Jesus as his Lord.

"One day as I walked through the living room where he was lying on the sofa, I went over and hugged him and said, 'I love you, Dad,'" she told me. "Tears came to his eyes—it was the first time I had ever seen him cry. As I began to share with him about the Lord, I could tell that the Holy Spirit had already prepared his heart. He willingly accepted Jesus right then!"

This is a classic case of a person being deceived by evil spirits to believe God is his enemy. But his eyes were opened to the truth when spiritual warfare was done on his behalf. Realizing God truly was his friend, he repented.

The enemy often attacks women by destroying their marriages, thus causing their children to grow up in one-parent homes. Psychologist Richard Dobbins reviews the damage Satan has done in this area:

Out of the materialism of the 1950s, the narcissism of the 1960s, and the hedonism of the 1970s has risen a society that aborts its unborn, commercializes the care of its children, and warehouses its elderly. Blinded by such confused priorities, we are dehumanizing our country and destroying our family relationships. . . .

Millions of broken families lie strewn across our land by a flagrant disregard for the sanctity of marriage and by selfishly sought divorces. Divorced mothers and their children comprise the largest group falling below the poverty line each year. Rising numbers of children in father-absent families are crippled in their search for a heterosexual identity.[7]

Rena, a pastor's daughter who grew up in church, suffered one such attack. She fought hard for her thirteen-year marriage to Jack, her high school sweetheart. She even resigned her position as minister of music at their church because he felt threatened by her being in the public eye. But he was "in love" with a nineteen-year-old girl who worked for him, and he wanted a divorce.

Rena told us:

I was an emotional mess. I never dreamed our ideal marriage could crumble. When problems developed, I tried to pray. My two boys needed a daddy, and I needed a husband. But I realized I really didn't know how to pray. I knew all the Bible stories, but I had no grasp of the principles in the Word and certainly no knowledge of the enemy.

I remember teaching a Bible study on Mary and Martha and realizing that with all my church work, I was a Martha. I prayed earnestly, *God, I really want to know You more.* I had no idea what I would go through as He answered that prayer.

I could do nothing to persuade Jack to change his mind. He wanted a quickie divorce, but I refused. It was two years before the divorce was granted. In the end his drinking and lifestyle led to the loss of his business, and he didn't even marry the girl he'd had the affair with.

Without the Lord's help I wouldn't have made it. He put a person here and a person there to pray for me and give me helpful books. I learned to pray the Word over my family, and I learned the value of praise. Sitting at the piano, I would play and sing to the Lord, and it was very healing.

After several years Rena met and married Trent, a man with two sons whose wife had abandoned them. Together they prayed and sought God's help for blending their children into a loving family, and they learned much about spiritual warfare in the process. It was not an easy road, but God was faithful to see them through, and today Rena and Trent are in full-time ministry together.

"God continues to answer my prayer to know Him more, and He's doing that for all of us," she says with a smile. "All four of our sons are serving the Lord—one works with us in the ministry, three of them are married to godly women and we have two beautiful grandchildren. He has given us joy and peace in ways I couldn't have dreamed possible."

We women *can* triumph if we choose to employ God's provision and obey His instructions. In the next chapter, we will examine the specially designed spiritual wardrobe and weaponry God has prepared for us.

Prayer

Lord, I pray that You will increase my ability to recognize the enemy's attacks and help me to take a stand against his strategies. Protect me from being deceived, and give me greater understanding of how I can stand in the gap on behalf of my loved ones who are under attack. Thank You for being with me continually. Amen.

3

What Our Spiritual Wardrobe Should Look Like

Therefore put on the complete armour of God, so that you may be able to stand your ground on the day of battle, and, having fought to the end, to remain victors on the field. Stand therefore, first fastening round you the girdle of truth and putting on the breastplate of uprightness as well as the shoes of the Good News of peace—a firm foundation for your feet. And besides all these take the great shield of faith, on which you will be able to quench all the flaming darts of the Wicked one; and take the helmet of salvation, and the sword of the Spirit which is the word of God. Pray with unceasing prayer and entreaty on every fitting occasion in the Spirit, and be always on the alert to seize opportunities for doing so, with unwearied persistence and entreaty on behalf of all God's people.

Ephesians 6:13–18 WEYMOUTH

When we were little girls and played "dress up," we would carefully choose what we put on—from the right shoes to the cutest hat. As grown women, we still like to dress in our best clothes for

37

a special event. But as Christians, we should consider our spiritual wardrobe the most important attire we will ever need to wear. Let's look at *what* it is and *why* we need to be clothed in it daily.

Ephesians 6:13–18 is Paul's warfare handbook—a basic-training manual—for the churches he had founded. He wanted to prepare them for the persecution and adversity he knew would come. Today, this passage is still the best description of the protective gear and weapons with which we equip ourselves for spiritual conflict.

William Gurnall, a seventeenth-century scholar, wrote:

> It is not left to everyone's fancy to bring whatever weapons he pleases; this would only breed chaos. . . . Look closely at the label to see whether the armor you wear is the workmanship of God or not. There are many imitations on the market nowadays. . . . Do not dare to call anything the armor of God which does not glorify Him and defend you against the power of Satan.[1]

The armor Paul speaks of is for our defense and protection against evil powers, but God also provides offensive weapons. Our warfare wardrobe is complete in every detail. However, it is our responsibility to put it on and to use it.

As mentioned earlier, a surprising number of Christians do not believe that our spiritual adversary is an actual entity, which of course defies the truth of Scripture (see Luke 4:1–13; Ephesians 6:12). Think how dangerous it would be to live in a war zone but refuse to acknowledge the reality of an enemy or his threat to one's survival! Yet that is the state of denial we see many believers in today. It is time for a wake-up call.

The Girdle of Truth

The girdle Paul refers to in the Ephesians 6 passage was actually a wide metal or leather belt worn by a soldier around his lower trunk to hold his armor tightly against his body and to support his sword. It was also used to carry money and other valuables. To "gird up your loins" was to prepare for action (see 1 Samuel 25:13 KJV).

Relating this to spiritual warfare, consider the role truth plays as the very essence of the Gospel—God's plan to free us from sin's bondage through His Son's sacrificial death, burial and resurrection. Jesus said, "Then you will know the truth, and the truth will set you free" (John 8:32).

Gurnall wrote, "If a person's understanding is clear in its hold on truth and his will is sincerely grounded in holy purposes, then he is a maturing Christian."[2] He warned that Satan, as a serpent, assails the truth by sending false teachers who sow error. Or as a lion, he sends persecutors who threaten danger or death in trying to force the believer to deny the truth.

Satan first assaulted the truth in the Garden when he asked Eve, "Did God really say . . . ?" (Genesis 3:1). Not having the belt of truth for armor, she wavered and began to doubt what God had said. Our enemy still uses this subtle weapon of doubt against us. It is "the truth that is in Jesus" (Ephesians 4:21) that we must fasten on tightly to protect us from the strategies of the evil one.

Nell's belt of truth slipped when she became fascinated with New Age holistic health and diets. Though she had a Christian upbringing, her pursuit of what she thought was truth soon ensnared her to become involved in a New Age cult.

Her mother, visiting from out of state and discovering the deception, challenged the young man who had lured Nell into the cult group. "My daughter once made a commitment to the Lord Jesus Christ, and she *will* come back to Him and forsake all this garbage you have exposed her to," she told him. "By the power and authority of the blood of Jesus, I bind every influence of Satan you have over my daughter."

When Nell heard about this confrontation, she told her mom, "I want to live my own life, so you and Dad back off my case."

"Honey, we love you too much to let the devil keep you in his clutches," her mom responded. "We'll battle Satan with everything that's in us until the god of this world stops blinding you to the truth and your will is freed to return to Jesus."

Nell's parents did spiritual warfare every day, commanding Satan to release her. They asked God to place a hedge of protection around her and bring to her remembrance all of the truth she had learned as a young girl. They praised the Lord for being a covenant-keeping God to those who love Him and keep His commandments. They enlisted friends in both states to pray.

One day Nell wandered into a Christian bookstore to buy some health-food cookbooks.

"As I was leaving, the store owner insisted I buy a little book, so I did just to get him to leave me alone," she reported. "Later that night I flipped through it and noticed it was full of Scripture verses. The author suggested reading those verses three times a day, like you would take vitamins. I was into anything that would make me healthier, so I did it. Before long those Scripture verses became more important to me than any of the cookbooks or the teachings of the cult."

Five months from the time her parents began spiritual warfare, Nell called them and asked if she could move back home and start life over again with Jesus. She has since graduated from a Bible school and has ministered in several countries, and today she is training her own children in spiritual warfare.

"How easy it was to get deceived when I stopped going to church, praying every day and reading my Bible," she admits. "But, thank God, my eyes were opened to the truth."

The Breastplate of Righteousness

The breastplate was a piece of armor that protected the soldier's heart and other vital organs (today's equivalent would be the bulletproof vest). It was fastened to the girdle, or belt, so it was held securely in place. Just as the ancient soldier knew it was critical for these two pieces of armor to be joined, it is important for us to remember that truth and righteousness always go together. *Righteousness* simply means "right action," "uprightness" or "conformity to the will of God."[3]

"Watch over your heart with all diligence, for from it flow the springs of life," advised Solomon (Proverbs 4:23 NASB). Satan often tempts us to compromise our standard of righteousness with such arguments as "But it's for a good cause" or "No one will ever know." The enemy knows that if we compromise the truth and accept his lies, he will gain a foothold in our lives. William Gurnall wrote:

> Righteousness and holiness are God's protection to defend the believer's conscience from all wounds inflicted by sin. . . . Your holiness is what the devil wants to steal from you. . . . He will allow a man to have anything, or be anything, rather than be truly and powerfully holy.[4]

Ruth is a friend who left her government job because she heard God's call to full-time missions work, but when she arrived on the field, she found that her senior missionary was misusing funds. Ruth had a dilemma: Should she quietly excuse this behavior, or should she stand on principle and risk her friendships, her own credibility and her future in missions? Ruth did the latter for one big reason: She wanted to please God more than she wanted to please people (see Galatians 1:10).

"I was shocked to discover how the devil will work through weak Christians," she said. "It was a very difficult time. Some of my friends thought I was just getting into a power struggle.

41

But I knew that to compromise on this issue to please people would mean displeasing God. Nothing is worth that. I left that organization but continued working in missions, and God met all my needs. The Lord helped me to forgive that woman, and then I 'locked it out with love,' so the enemy couldn't keep bringing the struggle back."

The devil knows the areas where you are vulnerable to compromise in your family relationships, in a job situation, in a friendship or in your church or prayer group. He will make it seem logical and in your own and others' best interests for you to bend your principles a bit.

Speaking to believers, James wrote, "Wash your hands, you sinners, and purify your hearts, you double-minded" (James 4:8). The compromising hearts of God's people—which is a form of spiritual adultery—was and no doubt still is God's greatest grief (see Hebrews 3:10). It is a subtle trap, indeed. But the soldier who always has his or her breastplate of righteousness firmly in place, secured by the belt of truth, will be protected from a divided heart.

The Gospel Shoes of Peace

Putting on one's shoes is a symbol of readiness. In Paul's day, shoes were not worn indoors (and still are not in many Eastern cultures). To put on your shoes indicated you were going outside the protection of the house. God told His people to eat the Passover with their shoes on so that they would be ready to flee Egypt (see Exodus 12:11). The soldier's shoes protected his feet and usually were fitted with metal cleats to make him more sure-footed in combat.

One commentator notes that the word translated *shod* in the New King James Version of Ephesians 6:15 comes from a compound Greek word meaning "binding something very tightly on the bottom of one's feet."[5] He continues with this observation:

> Paul uses this illustration to tell us that we must firmly tie *God's peace* onto our lives. . . . If we only give peace a loosely fitting position in our lives, it won't be long before the affairs of life knock our peace out of place. Hence, we must *bind* peace onto our minds and emotions in the same way Roman soldiers made sure to *bind* their shoes very tightly onto their feet. . . . [Thus] you will be empowered to keep marching ahead, impervious to the devil's attempts to take you down![6]

This important piece of the Christian's armor is crucial when navigating through the war zone of life. For instance, Joyce's shoes of peace enabled her to walk serenely through the "minefield" of her husband's wrath.

During a visit to her parents' home, Joyce and Barry were alone in the house one day when he went to take a shower. Because Joyce was running the washing machine, Barry got a burst of cold water that threw him into an unreasonable rage. Forgetting that the bathroom door was ajar and that Joyce was within earshot, he began screaming curses at her and calling her names. It was a gush of profanity that seemed demonic.

Joyce immediately began calling on God, asking, *Lord, how do I handle this?* She went to the living room and began running the vacuum cleaner while she prayed and bound the spirits of hatred and rage.

"I felt the Lord tell me, *Walk in the opposite spirit*," she said. "Barry was operating in a spirit of hate and condemnation; I needed to operate in a spirit of love and forgiveness. I forgave Barry for the cutting things he had said. By the time he came out of the bathroom, I truly had received God's peace."

As Barry was leaving to go wash his car, Joyce offered to go along and help.

"I cleaned all the windows on his car, inside and out, and he had no clue that he had upset me," she said. "When we got back to the house, I confronted him with what I had heard. I was able to stand my ground and do it calmly. He didn't apologize or express any regret whatsoever. He just glared at me and said, 'I didn't know you heard,' and walked away. That experience showed me just how hardened his heart had become, but it also showed me that God's peace can sustain me no matter what happens."

We have the assurance of Scripture that "the peace of God, which transcends all understanding, will guard [our] hearts and [our] minds in Christ Jesus" (Philippians 4:7).

The Shield of Faith

Various kinds of shields were in use in Paul's day, but the specific one Paul refers to in Ephesians 6 is the large rectangular shield that could protect the entire body. It was common practice for the soldier to anoint his shield with oil so that it would reflect the sun's rays and blind the enemy, and this would also help deflect the enemy's blows.

Gurnall gave this insight concerning the shield:

> The apostle compares faith to a shield because . . . the shield is intended for the defense of the whole body. . . . And if the shield was not large enough to cover every part at once, the skillful soldier could turn it this way or that way, to stop the swords or the arrows, no matter where they were directed. . . . Not only does the shield defend the whole body, but it defends the soldier's other armor also. . . . Every grace derives its safety from faith; each one lies secure under the shadow of faith.[7]

Concerning this shield of faith, it is important that we have faith in God—not faith in faith. Our confidence in God must be based on His character and trustworthiness, not on our ability to follow a formula. Scripture tells us, "Without faith it is impossible to please God, because anyone who comes to him must believe that he exists and that he rewards those who earnestly seek him" (Hebrews 11:6).

Chris is someone who has learned the importance of being protected by the shield of faith. Because she grew up in a dysfunctional family and suffered abuse as a child, she was tormented with thoughts of suicide, even after she became a Christian. Through prayer and counseling, the oppression lifted, and she was free.

"Then I learned that the enemy always tests your deliverance," she said. "Though I knew the Holy Spirit had powerfully ministered to me, I would occasionally have thoughts of suicide again. I had to use the shield of faith to deflect those fiery darts. Over and over I would say to the enemy, 'Satan, I resist you. I *have* been delivered in Jesus' name. I will live and not die. You are defeated, and I command you to flee.' I persisted until the enemy finally stopped bothering me in that area. I am totally free."

The foundation of our faith is in Scripture: "Faith comes by hearing, and hearing by the word of God" (Romans 10:17 NKJV). So the more thoroughly we are immersed in God's Word, the stronger our faith will be. By declaring aloud the promises of Scripture during prayer times, we can strengthen our faith as we hear those declarations. Simply put, faith means believing that God is who He says He is and that He will do what He says He will do.

The Helmet of Salvation

The helmet not only protected the soldier's head in battle but also bore an insignia or symbols identifying the army to which he belonged. Paul instructed, "Let us be sober, putting on . . . the hope of salvation as a helmet" (1 Thessalonians 5:8). This hope, or helmet, of salvation protects the Christian against attacks on the mind, one of Satan's primary targets.

To deal with such an attack, we must learn to distinguish the voice of our enemy from God's voice. God will speak words of love, comfort, conviction and guidance. The enemy speaks words of fear, accusation and condemnation.

Gwen's story is an example of how to repel Satan's attack on the mind. She, her husband and their thirteen-year-old grandson, Mark, were in their van heading home after a holiday visit to relatives. What had been a wonderful visit had gone sour just as they were saying their good-byes. Mark had been playing outdoors with his young cousins, one of whom got slightly hurt in a moment of Mark's carelessness. The child's mother gave Mark a tongue-lashing and embarrassed him in front of everyone.

With sagging spirits, the three of them got into the van to begin their eight-hundred-mile journey in miserable silence. Mark slumped on the seat as far back in the van as he could get. As they rode along, Gwen glanced out her window and saw a reflection of herself in the glass. In her mind she heard a voice say, *You're old and fat and ugly.* Studying the image for a moment, she thought to herself, *It's true, Gwen. You are old and fat and ugly.*

But suddenly she had a flash of insight. *That's a spirit of rejection!* she realized. *It came in with Mark, and it will stay with us all the way home if I permit it to.*

"I immediately bound the spirit of rejection and commanded it to flee, and then I prayed quietly," she reported. "In a very short time the whole atmosphere inside the van changed. Mark clambered up close to the front seat and began laughing and talking with us, and we enjoyed the trip home together. Had I not resisted that attack against my mind, I would have played right into the enemy's hand."

Dean Sherman's analogy is helpful:

> Every military post has guards. They stand quietly at their posts until they hear a rustling in the bushes. Then they immediately ask: "Who goes there?" and are prepared to evict any intruder. We too need to post a guard at the gate of our minds to check the credentials of every thought and every imagination, ready to cast down that which is not true, not righteous, or not of God. If it doesn't belong, out it goes. This is spiritual warfare: being alert to every thought.[8]

The Sword of the Spirit

The sword is used not only to defend against the enemy but also to offensively attack him. Paul's sword is the Word of God—the *rhema*. W. E. Vine says:

> The significance of *rhema* (as distinct from *logos*) is exemplified in the injunction to take "the sword of the Spirit, which is the word of God" (Ephesians 6:17); here the reference is not to the whole Bible as such, but to the individual Scripture which the Spirit brings to our remembrance for use in time of need, a prerequisite being the regular storing of the mind with Scripture.[9]

Lynn used the sword of the Spirit to resist a physical assault. As she was getting ready for bed one night while her husband, Jay, took the babysitter home, she felt an urge to pray, not knowing why. *Lord, what is this I'm feeling?* she asked. *Show me how to pray.*

Pray against a spirit of harassment, responded that still, small voice. She prayed accordingly, and after feeling a sense of release, she got into bed.

Within a few minutes, she heard people coming up the stairs. *Who is Jay bringing home with him at this hour?* she wondered.

The next thing she knew, a strange man knelt beside her bed and pressed a pistol to her neck. His companion, holding Jay at gunpoint, ripped out the phone cord.

"Just do as he says, Lynn," Jay said to her quietly, "and everything will be all right."

"Give me your rings," commanded the thief as he began trying to pull them off Lynn's finger.

Forgetting Jay's advice, Lynn answered, "No! In Jesus' name, you can't have my wedding rings!"

She reported:

Then his hands drew near to touch my body. Thoughts of rape, blood and even death entered my mind. As quickly as those thoughts came, Scriptures flowed into my heart. Although I was shaking, the promises of God filled my spirit, and total peace flooded my being. Repeatedly the man drew near, and it was as if an invisible force prevented him from going any further.

I lay crying softly in bed, with the gun still pointed to my throat, marveling that my two small children and baby were sleeping soundly and that my emotions hadn't carried me into a screaming, terrified frenzy. The other burglar went through the house, gathering whatever he thought had any value. After what seemed forever, the man backed away from my bedside, left the room and closed the door.

After waiting for some time, Lynn and Jay crept out to survey what was left of their plundered home. To their surprise, they found all their belongings piled on the living-room floor. Only a few pieces of jewelry were missing. Lynn and Jay wondered whether God had sent some noise, or perhaps an angel, to scare the thieves away. To this day, the mystery remains.

Lynn said, "Jay had established the habit of praying aloud every time we left our house or car, *Lord, please station Your angels to guard and protect our belongings.* God proved to us once again that He alone is our security."

Lynn's "secret weapon" was the arsenal of Scriptures—the sword of the Spirit—she had stored up in her heart, which kept her at peace in the midst of the attack. Clearly, the angels must have done battle on their behalf!

As another example, Josette had an opportunity to use the sword of the Spirit as an offensive weapon when her son, Troy, began having difficulty with his boss on his new job and called home for prayer. Using verses from Daniel, Josette began to pray, *Father, may Troy find favor and compassion with his boss. May he be well informed, quick to understand and qualified for the job. May he be found ten times better than others.* (See Daniel 1:4, 9, 20.)

Her warfare continued: *Satan, I block your tactics with the Word of God. My son is a mighty man of valor. God promises him prosperity. I bind the spirits of pride and jealousy in his boss that are coming against Troy. You will not hinder God's plan for him. Thank You, Lord, that Troy will be Your representative on this job and that he is becoming the man of God You created him to be.*

Josette continued praying in this way as the Lord gave her additional Scriptures, and Troy's situation gradually improved. Fourteen months later, when Troy was promoted to a job in another city, his boss gave him a farewell party and bragged about how qualified and well-informed Troy was in his work—a specific answer to his mother's prayers that were rooted in the Scriptures.

As many people's experiences attest, the Word of God is not only a spiritual weapon but also a source of great comfort. Arthur Mathews presents this challenge:

> If we accept the fact that our role in life is that of soldiers, then we must drop our toys and become more acquainted with the

weapons of our warfare. In a conflict situation a soldier's best friend is his weapon, because it is his one resource for disposing of the enemy, securing his own safety, and accomplishing the will of his captain.[10]

He then quotes missionary Amy Carmichael:

The only thing that matters is to throw all the energies of our being into the faithful use of this precious blade. Then, and only then, may we "rest our cause upon His Holy Word."[11]

For as long as we are on this earth, we will need to wear our armor and wield our sword. As William Gurnall wrote so concisely, "Once [the Christian] enters the gates of that glorious city, he can say, 'Armor was for earth but robes are for heaven.'"[12]

Prayer

Lord, I am so grateful for the armor You provide to protect us from the enemy. Help me to gain a deeper understanding of the power of the Word, our principal weapon, as I build up an arsenal of Scriptures to use in warfare. Because I know You are with me, I declare the enemy's plans will come to nothing. Amen.

4

How Strong Can a Woman Be?

The Lord gives the word [of power]; the women who bear and publish [the news] are a great host.

Psalm 68:11 AMPC

Ten thousand people were asked in a poll, "Who has had the most positive influence on your religious faith?" The most frequent answer from every age group was "My mother." The second-place response from men was "My wife." The survey also revealed that women have a higher faith level than men.[1] This poll simply proves what most of us knew all along: Women have a great deal of influence for God—which is both a privilege and a responsibility!

In Psalm 68:11, the word *women* is sometimes rendered *company*, which is a military word. But this is not a conventional company of women soldiers. A loose translation of the verse would be, "The women who proclaim the news of victory are an army of praisers." We women may be considered less muscular than men, but our praising, praying and proclaiming of the Good News have the power to push back the forces that seek to destroy our loved ones and our communities.

Why is it that we are so influential? One theory is that because women were created to give birth in the natural realm, we know more about travailing and giving birth in the spiritual realm. We tend to feel things deeply, are readily moved with compassion and have a high tolerance for pain. Women warriors have the tenacity to stick it out until the birthing is done and loved ones are brought from darkness into the light of Jesus.

"The hand that rocks the cradle is the hand that rules the world," wrote poet William Ross Wallace. We could paraphrase his thought, "The one who gives birth in the spiritual realm is the one who prevails over the powers of darkness."

Hurling Stones at the Enemy

We have all heard stories of women who performed feats of superhuman strength, such as lifting the back of a car when a child was in danger. The maternal instinct sends a surge of adrenaline through a woman, empowering her to do something thought impossible even for a well-muscled man. How much greater is the power the Holy Spirit gives to enable us in spiritual warfare!

Edith, a petite, graying mother, was puttering around her kitchen around 9:30 one Friday morning when a cold chill swept over her. Fear gripped her heart. *Dale is in danger*, a voice said inside her. She immediately began praying for her engineer son. Five . . . ten . . . fifteen minutes she prayed. Then the burden lifted, and she went back to washing dishes.

That evening, Dale called to tell her about his day. Around 9:30 that morning, while inspecting some remodeling work in the manufacturing plant where he worked, he suddenly felt an urge to move out of the way. As he stepped aside, a huge steel beam fell to the floor, striking the very spot where he had been standing seconds before.

In the natural realm, Dale's little mom never could have deflected the fall of that steel beam. But because Edith was sensitive to the voice of the Holy Spirit as she worked in her kitchen that morning, her son's life was spared.

Edith's story brings to mind the Old Testament account of the Israelite woman who, when she saw King Abimelech approaching her city to burn it, took immediate action. Watching him from the top of the tower of Thebez, she grabbed an upper millstone and hurled it down on the wicked king's head. Too proud to have it said that a woman killed him, the king ordered his armor bearer to draw his sword and finish him off (see Judges 9:50–54; 2 Samuel 11:21).

Never let it be said that women are weak! They are still hurling stones at the enemy's plans. This unnamed woman of Thebez is one of a large company of women who continue to wreak havoc on Satan's plans today.

Standing against the Flood

I (Ruthanne) learned years ago during a crisis how strong a woman can be, though I did not feel strong at the time. For months I had been studying about spiritual warfare and learning about our authority in Christ, but I was yet to put this truth to the test.

One October day when heavy rains hit our area, local radio stations warned of flash flooding. That afternoon it was time for me to drive the carpool to pick up kids from school, but my husband volunteered to go instead because of the bad weather. Just after he left, the rain began to fall even harder, thundering like Niagara Falls. Looking out the front door, I saw that water had filled the street and was now pouring over the curb, down our sloping yard toward the house. Muddy water flooded the sidewalk and was quickly rising to porch level.

In a panic, I tried to brace a board across the porch entrance and then laid towels over the threshold of the front door. In seconds, the rising water swept the board away and crept onto our small porch.

Suddenly I felt a righteous anger in my spirit and realized I needed to take authority over the enemy's attempt to damage our home. With no time to call my prayer partner or look up a Scripture verse, I just had to wing it.

"Devil, in the name of Jesus, I forbid you to enter this house with muddy floodwater," I shouted into the storm as I stood at the open front door. "This house belongs to God. It has been dedicated to Him, and you have no right to enter and destroy it. In Jesus' name, I command this water to recede."

When I stopped shouting, I realized the thundering noise had diminished and the rain was slackening. The water had come up to the threshold, and the towels were wet. But as I watched, the floodwater receded from the porch, formed a whirlpool below the step, and then ran down the walkway, around the corner of the house and down the driveway.

For a moment I stood rooted to the spot, almost in shock that my desperate tactic had worked. Then I began to praise God for His faithfulness, acknowledging that He had given the victory. My husband and son were amazed when they got home and saw the mud silt on the porch that confirmed my story.

The following year we had another season of heavy rain with flash-flood warnings. I began taking authority over the devil as soon as I heard the news, declaring our home off-limits to his destructive work. Though we had more rain that week than had fallen the previous October, floodwaters never threatened our house again. I learned the effectiveness of engaging in spiritual warfare before a situation reaches crisis proportions.

Of course, we have no power on our own; we must rely on the Holy Spirit's power. But operating in faith, not fear, is one way to overcome the enemy's harassment. I might add that I do not believe we are to indiscriminately "take authority" over the weather. (In fact, in this case I did not command the rain to cease.) But this kind of action is appropriate in situations when we are led by the Holy Spirit.

Now that I live in a different part of Texas, one where drought is a common problem, we often pray for rain. But when bad storms threaten, I ask the Lord to send the needed rain without any destruction to life or property.

Battling for a Woman's Heart

What can one woman do? We have already looked at Deborah and the difference she made in the nation of Israel. Scripture gives many more accounts of women who wielded godly influence in significant ways: Jochebed, Shiphrah, Puah, Miriam, Hannah, Huldah, Esther, Ruth, Elizabeth, Mary, Anna, Dorcas, Priscilla, Phoebe and Joanna, among others.

It should also be noted that the godly influence of these women was not always given through prayer alone. Sometimes prayer *plus* action was needed. This holds true for today.

Laura, a Nebraska farmer's wife, models one such woman. Her commitment to prayer and action has changed many people's lives. Bonnie was one of them. With a hardworking husband, two children, a home and a few friends, Bonnie seemed to have everything required for happiness. But because of childhood molestation, she had allowed the seeds of hatred toward men to grow in her heart. Turning to other women for love and acceptance, she had gotten involved in lesbianism.

Bonnie had become a Christian and gotten married, but she still struggled with affections for her former lovers. She even preferred to dress like a male. But her ambivalent feelings made her so miserable that she came to Laura for help.

Laura prayed with Bonnie and shared Scriptures that address God's opposition to that behavior (see Leviticus 18:22; Romans 1:26–31; 1 Corinthians 6:9). At first Bonnie had a hard time accepting what Laura shared. But after several hours of receiving Laura's teaching and prayer, Bonnie prayed a simple prayer: "God, forgive me. I see it as sin."

Finally, Bonnie began to sob as the healing power of Jesus' forgiveness engulfed her. Soon afterward, when Laura took her to a women's conference, Bonnie experienced godly love, acceptance and affection from women. A new life of freedom began for her.

Laura remained a strong force of encouragement in Bonnie's life, showing Bonnie that she could have a healthy relationship with a female friend. Laura helped Bonnie redecorate her home; then they worked on her appearance—hairstyle, makeup and clothes. Laura and her husband helped Bonnie plant a garden. When Bonnie's husband returned from an out-of-state job assignment, he hardly recognized his wife. But he liked the changes, and so did she.

Because Laura persevered in prayer and action to help a friend who had asked for help with a struggle, she was richly rewarded when Bonnie broke through to freedom from the conflict that had tormented her.

Enlarging Our Borders

Perhaps you feel your circle of influence is pretty small, consisting of your husband, your children, their school, your extended family, your church and your friends. If you are single, your sphere may consist primarily of your work relationships, your family, your friends and your church. If you are an empty nester or a widow, you may feel your world is shrinking.

Have you ever considered that God might want to expand your horizon? That He might want to use you to pray not only for your family and friends, but also for your city, state, nation or another nation of the world?

I (Quin) remember how God began enlarging my borders some years ago. My husband's job had taken us to a different town, which I did not like very well. I complained to the Lord about it one day. Later, in my morning Bible reading, I stumbled across Jeremiah's message to God's people living in exile. It jumped from the page into my heart: "Build houses and settle down. . . . Seek the peace and prosperity of the city to which I have carried you into exile. Pray to the LORD for it, because if it prospers, you too will prosper" (Jeremiah 29:5, 7).

Pray for the city where God had brought me? How could I? Where would I start? Because I knew nothing about spiritual warfare in those days, I began by praying about things I read in the daily newspaper. Not a bad place to start, really.

A year later we moved to another area. In my Bible reading one day, verses from Isaiah sprang to life and challenged me to begin praying for the new city where I now lived. The passage said:

> I have set watchmen upon your walls, O Jerusalem, who will never hold their peace day or night; you who [are His servants and by your prayers] put the Lord in remembrance [of His promises], keep not silence, and give Him no rest until He establishes Jerusalem and makes her a praise in the earth.
>
> Isaiah 62:6–7 AMPC

In place of *Jerusalem*, I put the name of my city. And I wrote in my Bible, "God wants to station me as an intercessor sentry—a guard to watch in prayer for my family and city. I'll need God's strategy to ambush the enemy's plan."

I did some research on our sprawling resort area, and one day after fasting and prayer, a friend and I took a prayer walk in a two-block area of downtown. We passed an antique store with statues of Buddha in the window, a liquor store with a sign that read "In Booze We Trust," a New Age store with a window display of crystals and weird head sculptures, a secret lodge temple, a Native American museum and an amusement palace with huge carved foreign idols. Of course, not everything associated with Native American culture or other ethnic groups is demonic, but the enemy has infiltrated most cultures of the world. My heart was broken to see in only a two-block area so many things that surely were not honoring to God. Yet I realized that only a few years ago I had been ignorant of such traps of the enemy.

As my friend and I walked, we bound the enemy's works of darkness and deception and asked the Holy Spirit to bring a revelation of Jesus Christ to the hearts of the people. Later we walked up and down and prayed on nearby streets, where psychics, go-go dancers, nightclubs and liquor stores catered to summer tourists.

In time we enlisted other women who shared our vision to see righteousness become the standard for the city. Walking in pairs, we covered malls, schools, government buildings, residential neighborhoods, beaches and parks.

Over the next few months, a fortune-teller went out of business, one psychic shop shut down, and a teen nightclub closed its doors. We heard of other results later on, but of course we will not know the full effect of our spiritual warfare until we get to heaven. Though I have since moved from that city, my prayer partners continue standing against darkness there, and others are catching the vision that they can make a difference through prayer.

John Dawson, author of *Taking Our Cities for God,* writes:

The fact is, there is a battle raging over your city and it is affecting you right now. Our individual blind spots and vices are usually common to the culture around us, and that culture is influenced by what the Bible calls principalities and powers (Eph. 6:12). . . . Spiritual warfare begins at a personal level and escalates through layers of increasing difficulty—from personal and family to the realm of church life, and beyond that to the collective church in the city and the national and international realms.

Have you ever thought about the battle for your immediate neighborhood? . . . Several years ago my staff and I went on a prayer walk around our neighborhood. We stood in front of every house, rebuked Satan's work in Jesus' name and prayed for a revelation of Jesus in the life of each family. We are still praying. . . . At this writing there are at least nine Christian families in the block where I live, and there is a definite sense of the Lord's peace.[2]

I (Quin) applied John Dawson's advice later, when living out west near my young grandchildren. Some days when I pulled them around our neighborhood in a red wagon, we sang a made-up song: "Let the King of glory come here." It was a fun learning exercise for the kids, but later we saw results. One day, a neighbor I did not know knocked on our door and asked if we were Christians. She needed some spiritual help, and we were able to have a good conversation with her family. Yes, our borders can be enlarged when we are open to doing things that seem a bit "out of the box."

Prayer-walking your neighborhood or community may seem a simple exercise, but it can have a greater spiritual impact than you realize. One year, a women's group that I (Ruthanne) am part of organized a prayer drive that covered all the schools in the county. The teams would drive to a school, stand in the parking lot to pray and declare Scriptures, then drive to the next location.

Later, they planned prayer drives to cover major government institutions and offices. These were powerful Psalm 68:11 women!

Taking Back Our Nations

Nehemiah gives us an example of the impact of one person confessing the sins of his nation. When he learned that the enemy still had access to Jerusalem, some eight hundred miles away from where he was living in exile, he wept, mourned, fasted and prayed because of the condition of his homeland. He even confessed the sins of his forefathers (see Nehemiah 1:6–7). Then he took action, getting permission and funding to rally his people who were still living in Jerusalem to help rebuild the broken-down wall. They accomplished the task in record time, despite their enemies' opposition.

Might God be asking the same of you? If so, God will give you a prayer from His heart to pray in repentance for your nation. Here's how one woman in the United States chose to pray: "God, we are truly sorry for the way our nation has gone against Your biblical principles. Forgive us for the sins of abortion, same-sex marriages, lawlessness, bribery and discrimination and for passing laws that are contrary to Your commandments. Have mercy on us, forgive our sins, and help us restore our nation to one of righteousness."

Once on a prayer journey to Washington, I (Quin) joined more than four thousand Christian women for a two-hour prayer gathering in front of the U.S. Capitol building. First we prayed for our nation. We asked God to give wisdom, knowledge and understanding to all our government leaders. We engaged in warfare against principalities and powers of darkness that have allowed abortion on demand, racism, humanism in our schools, widespread drug abuse and an increase in crime, pornography, child abuse and missing children.

Then we prayed for the women of America—the married, the divorced, the widowed, the single. We prayed for working mothers, for abused wives, for the wives and women of the military. We asked God to minister to their deepest needs and reveal Himself to them.

We did not demonstrate or hold up signs; we just prayed. Afterward, small groups of women walked around the Capitol grounds, praying for those who work there, and then small groups of women did the same around the White House, the Supreme Court and various embassies. We prayed quietly for God's purposes to be accomplished in our nation.

It is meaningful to walk any ground where the devil is operating and to assault him and make an outward declaration of God's victory in that place. As Joshua was about to march into the Promised Land, God told him to do the same:

> "I will give you every place where you set your foot, as I promised Moses. . . . Be strong and courageous, because you will lead these people to inherit the land. . . . Do not be afraid; do not be discouraged, for the LORD your God will be with you wherever you go."
>
> Joshua 1:3, 6, 9

We can act upon this word today as the Holy Spirit shows us where to set our foot and enables us to keep an attitude of humility and repentance as we pursue such a prayer project.

Battling in the Heavenlies

A big obstacle for many women in maintaining a consistent prayer life is the nagging question, How can my prayers possibly make a difference in the way things turn out? One of Satan's biggest ploys is to dissuade us from pursuing prayer. Yet Scripture shows us that when believers pray on earth, they instigate activity in the heavenlies.

Daniel 10 describes the time the prophet Daniel had an angelic visitation after three weeks of praying, fasting and repenting on behalf of his people. The angel told Daniel that on the first day he humbled himself to pray, God had heard his words. In fact, the angel had been dispatched with a response to Daniel's prayer but had encountered interference from "the prince of the Persian kingdom" (Daniel 10:13). The messenger angel had to receive help from the angel Michael to get through. He then delivered a prophetic message to Daniel and indicated that on his return, he would fight both the prince of Persia and the prince of Greece (see verse 20).

If there were rulers (called princes) in the spiritual realm trying to stop Daniel's prayers from being answered, are we immune? No! Hostile spiritual forces—the principalities and powers Paul speaks of in Ephesians 6:12—still try to block our prayers from being answered. And Scripture implies that these evil princes rule over different geographical areas.

So, when you go on a prayer walk of your own, ask the Holy Spirit to reveal to you the spirits needing to be bound in that area. Then ask God to open blinded eyes so that people might turn from darkness to light and receive forgiveness through Jesus.

Empowered by the Comforter

The gift of the Holy Spirit empowers us to be strong women of God, even in our moments of weakness. Jesus promised His followers:

> "I will ask the Father, and He will give you another Comforter (Counselor, Helper, Intercessor, Advocate, Strengthener, and Standby), that He may remain with you forever—the Spirit of Truth. . . . He will teach you all things."
>
> John 14:16–17, 26 AMPC

Without this gift of the Holy Spirit, we would be powerless before the enemy. But He strengthens us for battle in many ways. The Holy Spirit:

- Testifies of Jesus (see John 15:26; Romans 8:16).
- Teaches (see Luke 12:12; 1 Corinthians 2:13).
- Guides (see Matthew 10:19–20; John 16:13).
- Reveals (see John 14:20; 1 Corinthians 2:9–10).
- Comforts (see John 14:26 AMPC; Acts 9:31).
- Gives joy (see John 15:11; Romans 14:17).
- Gives spiritual gifts (see 1 Corinthians 12:4–31).
- Liberates (see John 8:32; Romans 8:2).
- Empowers for service (see Luke 4:14; Acts 1:8).
- Intercedes for us (see Romans 8:26; 1 Corinthians 14:14–15).

Many believe that when we ask the Holy Spirit to intercede through us, we are to seek God's will and then pray accordingly. Still others believe it involves praying in an unknown tongue, as those in the early Christian church did. Of course both ideas are valid, and it is important to discuss this particular "weapon." Consider Paul's words:

> The Spirit also helps our weakness; for we do not know how to pray as we should, but the Spirit Himself intercedes for us with groanings too deep for words; and He who searches the hearts knows what the mind of the Spirit is, because He intercedes for the saints according to the will of God.
>
> Romans 8:26–27 NASB

> I will pray with the spirit, and I will pray with the understanding also.
>
> 1 Corinthians 14:15 KJV

Interceding according to the will of God is the most important ingredient of prayer and the key to effectiveness. Pastor Judson Cornwall explains the use of tongues in prayer:

> Prayer is the most valuable use of tongues for it is "speaking to God."
>
> . . . The Holy Spirit is certainly not limited to the English language, nor is He confined to modern languages. He has access to every language ever used by mankind, and He is very familiar with the language used in heaven. When deep intercession is needed, the Spirit often uses a language that is beyond the intellectual grasp of the speaker to bypass the censorship of his or her conscious mind, thereby enabling the Spirit to say what needs to be prayed without arguing with the faith level of the one through whom the intercession flows.
>
> Praying in tongues is not the work of the subconscious. It's really supra-intellectual praying. That is, the prayer is beyond the natural mind, not beneath the conscious level. Intercessory prayer in tongues is not incoherent speech. The very words are motivated by the Holy Spirit, addressed to the Father, and approved by the Lord Jesus. (See Mark 16:17.)[3]

According to Acts 2:39, the gift is available to all born-again Christians—not just those who lived in the first century after Christ. The only requirements are that you be God's child and that you ask (see Luke 11:11–13). We should use the gift of praying in the Spirit not just during regular devotional times, but also whenever we sense a need for prayer as we go about our daily activities.

By now you have gotten the idea that every battle differs, as does the strategy for each battle. The Lord loves a tenacious warrior who is ready to take on an assignment at a moment's notice and who will seek His direction for strategy and timing. One friend suggests three principles to help us keep our warfare in proper perspective:

1. Aggression toward the enemy
2. Ruthlessness against our pride and selfishness
3. Tolerance and love toward one another

Thus we have an acrostic, the ART of spiritual warfare. How strong can a woman be? As strong as she will allow the Holy Spirit to be through her. But becoming that vessel the Holy Spirit can use requires discipline—and that is the topic of our next chapter.

Prayer

Thank You, Lord, for providing the power of the Holy Spirit to enable me to fulfill my prayer assignments. Please give me clear strategy and timing for every battle I face. Help me always to walk in humility and depend on Your strength and wisdom, not my own. I praise You, Lord—the captain of our salvation—for Your promise of victory. Amen.

5

The Disciplines of the Spirit-Empowered Woman

"For if you remain silent at this time, relief and deliverance for the Jews will arise from another place, but you and your father's family will perish. And who knows but that you have come to your royal position for such a time as this?" Then Esther sent this reply to Mordecai: . . . "I and my attendants will fast as you do. When this is done, I will go to the king. . . . And if I perish, I perish."

Esther 4:14–16

Queen Esther is a biblical example of how strong a woman can be. When facing a crisis that threatened the annihilation of the Jews, she called for a period of fasting and prayer before she took any action on her own. Then she put her life on the line by going to the king and intervening for her people's lives.

Perhaps the greatest lessons we can learn from Esther are *discipline* and *balance*. She did not rush to implement a plan of her own without seeking God's direction. Nor did she take a passive role and say, "If God wants to do something, He can do it." Disciplining herself and her people through a fast, she balanced that by taking action one step at a time.

Obedience

Esther's story provides an excellent model for fighting our tough spiritual battles. Long before she was selected as one of the candidates to be queen, Esther had learned the discipline of obedience. She willingly obeyed instructions from Mordecai, her foster father. Then she submitted to a disciplined year of preparation before she was presented to the king. Even after being crowned queen of Persia, she continued to follow Mordecai's godly counsel.

When Mordecai conveyed to her Haman's edict calling for all the Jews to be killed on a certain day, he asked her to go before the king and plead for mercy. Esther was reluctant to do so because such boldness could jeopardize her life, but Mordecai's appeal that perhaps she was now in the palace for this very purpose caused her to take the challenge. Shortly thereafter, she called for God's people to join her in three days of fasting. As the story unfolds, we see that Esther was following three important principles:

1. She settled in her heart that this battle was one in which she should be involved. She was in the palace "for such a time as this," and her commitment was solid.
2. She called the Jewish people to a fast, recognizing a solution was beyond her human wisdom. She would have to rely totally upon God.
3. She took action one step at a time, trusting God for His direction at each juncture.

God granted Esther favor when she went to the king unbidden; the king held out his scepter to receive her. But instead of immediately presenting her petition, Esther invited the king and Haman to a banquet she had prepared. At the table that evening, she still did not reveal her request, though the king gave her the opportunity. She was aware of the importance of timing. She asked the two men to come to another banquet the following day—but an amazing thing happened that night.

God intervened by giving the king a sleepless night and causing him to learn of a long-forgotten favor Mordecai had done for him. It was a case of God revealing at a critical moment something that had long been hidden.

Totally unaware of God's strategy, Esther simply had to keep her trust in Him. During the second banquet, Esther revealed to the king Haman's evil plot, and suddenly the tables were turned on him. Haman ended up being hung on the very gallows he had built for Mordecai, who was now honored as a hero (see Esther 6–9).

This was a victory far greater than Esther could have imagined. She did the possible while God did the seemingly impossible to reverse the curse against the Jews, and they were spared. In the end, Haman's entire estate was given to Esther, and Mordecai was promoted to second in command under the king.

Fasting

As we mentioned, Esther's immediate response to crisis was to call for a three-day fast in preparation for her going before the king. It seems quite plausible that during those three days, God revealed to her the strategy she was to follow. In like manner, fasting can become a weapon of warfare for us to receive God's guidance and strategy for our intercession and spiritual battles.

The prophetess Anna is an example of an intercessor who, like Esther, was in the right place at the right time. For years she had been in the Temple, ministering to the Lord with fasting and prayers.

One day the Spirit led Anna to enter a certain area of the Temple at the exact moment Mary and Joseph arrived with the infant Jesus. Recognizing that He was indeed the promised Messiah, Anna was the first woman to broadcast the Good News (see Luke 2:36–38). Her years of prayer and fasting were richly rewarded.

However, fasting is not limited to just being a way to wage spiritual warfare or a way to minister to the Lord. *Dake's Annotated Reference Bible* offers the view that fasting is also the antidote for unbelief:

> The disciples asked the Lord why they could not heal a lunatic boy. Jesus said, "Because of your unbelief. . . . Howbeit this kind goeth not out but by prayer and fasting" (Matthew 17:20–21 KJV). Faith needs prayer for its development and full growth, and prayer needs fasting for the same reason. This is a biblical doctrine. To fast means to abstain from food—that which caused the fall of man.
>
> Fasting humbles the soul before God, chastens the soul, and crucifies the appetites and denies them so as to give time to prayer. It manifests earnestness before God to the exclusion of all else, shows obedience, gives the digestive system a rest, demonstrates the mastery of man over appetites, aids in temptation, helps to attain power over demons, develops faith, crucifies unbelief, and aids in prayer.[1]

Some Christians are reluctant to fast because they fear it can lead to fanaticism or occultism. We are aware that fasting is practiced by spiritists and adherents of false religions to sharpen their sensitivities to the spiritual realm and even to invite demons to give them power. But Jesus spoke of fasting at the same time He taught His followers how to pray and how to give. All three are disciplines the Christian should observe (see Matthew 6:1–18).

In his excellent book *God's Chosen Fast*, Arthur Wallis writes:

> We must not think of fasting as a hunger strike designed to force God's hand and get our own way! Prayer, however, is more complex than simply asking a loving father to supply his child's needs. Prayer is warfare. Prayer is wrestling. There are opposing forces. There are spiritual cross currents. . . .
>
> The man who prays with fasting is giving heaven notice that he is truly in earnest; that he will not give up nor let God go without the blessing. . . .
>
> You should expect that a season of fasting would prove to be for you, as it was for your Master, a time of conflict with the powers of darkness. Satan will often try to take advantage of your physical condition to launch an attack. Discouragement is one of his weapons. Guard against it by maintaining a spirit of praise.[2]

We see that setting captives free also is a scriptural purpose for fasting. God asks, "Is not this the kind of fasting I have chosen: to loose the chains of injustice and untie the cords of the yoke, to set the oppressed free and break every yoke?" (Isaiah 58:6).

We see this in the story of Faye, whose teenage daughter Angie became ensnared by drug and alcohol abuse as well as sexual encounters. When this happened, Faye and her husband determined not to stop fasting and praying until she was free. Faye made enlarged copies of Scripture prayers from the first edition of this book and posted them all over her bedroom walls and mirror so she could pray them often.

"Whenever Angie brought her friends over, they would all notice the Scriptures and make fun of me," Faye said. "She had no idea how many meals her dad and I missed as we fasted while praying for her."

As a prophetic act, Faye got a heavy chain that represented Satan's hold on her daughter. She placed it on a concrete block and hammered at it with a brick, intending to break it. Striking the chain, she would say, "Satan, you loose your hold on my Angie. You cannot keep her in bondage to drugging and drinking. She *will* come back to the Lord Jesus, her Savior!"

Faye soon realized she could not break that heavy chain by herself but that she and her husband together could. "After we demolished it," she said, "we hung it on a hook in the garage as a reminder that Angie's bondage would be broken. It gave us courage to keep on believing for her freedom."

Daily, Faye reminded the Lord that they had trained their daughter in God's ways and that they fully expected her to return to Him (see Proverbs 22:6).

Angie's turnaround took about three years. When she did come back to the Lord, Angie told me (Quin), "My parents provided Christian role models to me—happy, never fighting, taking us to church and loving me. My mom was especially positive and peaceful. My dad was quick to defend her every time I screamed how much I hated her."

One Sunday soon after Angie's rededication, she stood before the church congregation and said, "I am fascinated with Jesus—absolutely fascinated." She went on to graduate with honors from college. Now, as a wife and mother of a daughter, she also holds down a very responsible job. At this writing she is even leading worship in their church. She lives near her parents, grandmother and a host of aunts and uncles who prayed for her during her rebellious years.

Regardless of how impossible your situation appears, it is important to keep your eyes on God, not just the problem. He can give you strategy for your battle. And as this story illustrates, fasting is an important discipline.[3]

While abstaining from all food for a season is the primary means of fasting, some cannot go completely without food for medical reasons. But there are many different ways to fast:

- Eat no solid food from sunup to sundown.
- Eat only vegetables and clear liquids.
- Take only bread and water.
- Take only clear liquids with no solid food.
- Drink only water.
- Abstain from all meat and/or "pleasant food" (Daniel 10:3 NKJV).
- Follow the "Esther fast," taking no food or water for three days (see Esther 4:16).
- Abstain from sweets or certain favorite foods or activities for a season while giving more time to prayer.

We suggest that you seek the Lord's guidance as to the type and length of fast you pursue, but beginning with shorter periods before attempting a prolonged fast is advisable. It is also advisable to consult your doctor before beginning any fast that drastically alters your diet. The point is that fasting, in whatever form, allows you to concentrate on prayer and Scripture. Often the Holy Spirit will speak to you through the Word to give correction or encouragement, as well as to give you strategy for the battles you are facing.

Hardship

While fasting is a discipline many Christians choose to ignore, there is another discipline that none of us can ignore: hardship and adversity. Paul wrote to Timothy, "You therefore must endure hardship as a good soldier of Jesus Christ. No one engaged in warfare entangles himself with the affairs of this life, that he may please him who enlisted him as a soldier" (2 Timothy 2:3–4 NKJV).

During a difficult period in my life many years ago, I (Ruthanne) developed the habit of walking a mile every day to talk to the Lord and settle my thoughts. I was dealing with a rebellious teenager, caring for my invalid in-laws living in our home and trying to cope with financial pressures and myriad problems while my husband traveled frequently. I struggled against self-pity and the feeling that I was shouldering the load alone.

On my walk one crisp October morning, the Lord spoke to me through Isaiah 45:3: "I will give you the treasures of darkness and hidden riches of secret places, that you may know that I, the LORD, who call you by your name, am the God of Israel" (NKJV).

Then He said very clearly, *Ruthanne, these are precious days. I am teaching you the treasures of darkness.*

I desperately wanted God to quickly solve all these problems—they certainly did not seem "precious" to my natural mind. Yet I knew they were not going to evaporate overnight. The Lord said He was teaching me as I allowed Him to—that there was value in the experience. Then I remembered reading about Jesus that "though He was a Son, yet He learned obedience by the things which He suffered" (Hebrews 5:8 NKJV).

After that morning with the Lord under the oak trees, my circumstances got worse, not better. But I began to see that from God's point of view, my response to the difficulties was more important than the problems themselves. He wanted to change me, not just my circumstances, and I finally yielded to His plan.

I have come to believe that God does His best work in darkness. We find this to be the case in the act of Creation, in the incarnation, in the Garden of Gethsemane, at Calvary and, yes, even in my own "dark night of the soul."

The glory of it all for me was not just seeing my circumstances change (they eventually did, though not in all the ways I had hoped for) but in allowing God to change me. That was the greater blessing. And in the process, I came to know God and His character and faithfulness as only adversity can teach us. In fact, it was during those years that I learned my most valuable lessons about the principles of spiritual warfare.

Captive Thoughts

All who enter the arena of spiritual warfare quickly learn that their mind is a battleground bombarded with doubt, discouragement, false accusations and mockery from Satan and his emissaries. But we can ask the Holy Spirit to empower us to take captive our false thoughts and to make them obedient to Christ. As Paul teaches, "We demolish arguments and every pretension that sets itself up against the knowledge of God, and we take captive every thought to make it obedient to Christ" (2 Corinthians 10:5).

Anita, who was active with an effective ministry of counseling, deliverance and teaching, learned firsthand how the enemy assaults our minds. Because of her parents' advanced age and failing health, she had to pull back from public ministry and move a thousand miles away to care for them. Although Anita knew this was God's plan for her, it was painful to leave her friends and prayer partners behind. In adjusting to becoming a caregiver, she had to learn to discipline her mind.

She said:

As time passed, I began to have more and more negative thoughts about everything—but especially about myself. I believed every "tear down" thought that wandered past. It seemed I couldn't trust myself to hear the Lord, and every negative Scripture in the Word seemed aimed at me. Down and down I went. No longer any balance—just negative.

I was finally fighting thoughts attacking my salvation. I couldn't pray, couldn't read the Word—and I didn't want to. Then one night the Lord told me to write a list of the good things about myself. I explained I had none, but He assured me He would show me this was untrue. And He began to give me the list.

I argued every point in the beginning. For example, He said I had compassion, while I could only feel the hardness of my heart. He went on to remind me of instances where I had shown compassion for Mom.

As we went on I had a thought: *Satan stands before the throne accusing believers* [see Revelation 12:10]. So that gives new meaning to the Scripture that tells us to think on the good things [see Philippians 4:8]. The good report is needed to balance the thrusts of the wicked one, for oneself as well as for others.

The Lord showed me that the mind is a battlefield. Enemy ammunition flies around, and we must learn to avoid it. If you caress it and claim it, it's yours. It is wise to counterattack with your own ammunition—the list of good things God has spoken to you, in addition to the written Word. Knowing that the Lord has given us spiritual weapons is so powerful for the tearing down of strongholds.

When the enemy returns, I can say, "Satan, the Lord says I do have compassion. I'll not receive the lies you are telling me." This has released me. Now I feel more comfortable going to the Word, not because I have to (which leads to guilt) but because the desire is there. Now I can more quickly smile, and I walk with less of a burden.

The assignment God gave Anita was not an easy one, but in the end it led to the salvation of both her parents. How grateful she was that she had obeyed!

Declarations

As we submit to these disciplines of prayer, fasting, patience in hardship and the control of our thoughts, we can become women warriors empowered by the Holy Spirit—and all that we do will be to the glory of God our Father.

Our friend Lou shared the struggle she had to discipline her tongue. Her elderly mother had moved from another city to the apartment behind Lou's house. In her difficult adjustment to new surroundings and attending a different church, Lou's mother would often vent her frustrations on her daughter.

One day when Lou was talking about plans for her next Sunday school lesson, her mother said, "Well, everyone doesn't teach Sunday school for the right reasons."

"Mother, I get the message," Lou snapped and then walked out of the room.

A few days later she shared the experience with her prayer partner, Nita, as they worked on plans for a church reception. "I know I need to control my tongue," Lou groaned, "but Mom's criticism just sets me off."

"When you said what you did, you received her message as if it were true," Nita reminded her. "You need to cancel those words and speak the truth instead. Let's go for a prayer walk while you begin to declare, 'I can do all things unto the glory of God.'"

As Lou made her declaration, she and Nita walked to the church fellowship hall to continue their planning. Upon entering the building, the first thing they saw was a dedication plaque on the wall with a large inscription: "Unto the glory of God."

"There's your confirmation," Nita said, laughing. "You just need to remember to keep declaring it!"

Discipline

"What is the most important thing you have learned through your experiences in spiritual warfare?" we asked a number of seasoned intercessors.

Many said *discipline*—that quality so essential to victory but so distasteful to the flesh. Who would not want to win in a skirmish with the enemy? Yet few of us easily submit to the discipline and dying to self that are necessary to overcome Satan's onslaughts.

"The enemy can use our own ignorance against us," one intercessor responded. "He knows the Law that will bring accusations to those who are trying to live up to its standard. We must discipline ourselves to learn God's Word and use it as a weapon against the attacks of the enemy."

Another wrote, "Probably the most significant lesson I learned was the importance of disciplining my tongue—no gossip, backbiting, silly talk, coarse jesting. In prayer and warfare, we should use our tongues according to the Word of God and allow the Holy Spirit to lead us in what we say to other people."

"I must always be prepared, try never to let my guard down," a third person said, "and listen continually for the voice of the Holy Spirit."

As we learned from Chris's story in chapter 3, it is important to discipline our minds so as not to entertain thoughts from the enemy, but rather to resist those thoughts with God's Word.

Anyone who has gone through conventional military training will tell you that discipline, obedience and persistence are critically important in producing a successful soldier. The same principles apply to our spiritual training.

Webster defines *discipline* as "training that corrects, molds, or perfects the mental faculties or moral character." Our yielding to the correcting, molding and perfecting work of the Holy Spirit can be painful, but it pays rich dividends by making us effective spiritual warriors.

Many modern-day Esthers and Annas have come to their "royal positions" for such a time as this. Discipline and balance— doing what we need to do to cooperate with God—are hallmarks of Spirit-empowered women. These are the women who success-fully use their weapons and find effective strategies for spiritual warfare—and that is our topic in the next chapter.

Prayer

Lord, I thank You for teaching us to pray specifically and with persistence, assuring us that when we ask, You hear. Help me to be disciplined, tenacious and faithful in prayer, always sensitive to the Holy Spirit's leading. Lord, forgive me for expecting You to answer according to my wishes and timetable. I know Your thoughts and Your ways are so much higher than mine [see Isaiah 55:8–9]. Help me to trust Your perfect timing, for I know You never make a mistake. Thank You for Your great faithfulness. Amen.

6

Our Weapons and Strategy

For though we live in the world, we do not wage war as the world does. The weapons we fight with are not the weapons of the world. On the contrary, they have divine power to demolish strongholds.

2 Corinthians 10:3–4

Put on God's whole armor . . . that you may be able successfully to stand up against [all] the strategies and the deceits of the devil.

Ephesians 6:11 AMPC

"In the name of Jesus, you give that purse back to me," Kay shouted as she chased a young teenager across the grocery-store parking lot. "I earned that money, and you have no right to it."

As Kay grabbed the scared kid by the arm and jerked her purse out of his hand, he broke down crying. It was his first time to try purse snatching as he had seen his older buddies do. But he picked the wrong young woman in this case—or the right one, depending on how you looked at it.

Kay knew she had authority in the name of Jesus, and she responded to the challenge without thinking of the possible dangers. She began sharing the Gospel with the youngster, explaining that he needed to accept Jesus as Savior and then trust God to provide him a job. He walked away visibly shaken.

"Kay, you could have gotten hurt!" I (Ruthanne) said when she shared the incident. A convert from the drug culture, Kay was attending the Bible school where my husband was a teacher. The store where she had stopped was a known trouble spot for thievery.

"I had just gotten paid at work, and I needed that money to pay my school bill," she said. "No way was I going to let the devil steal from me!"

Later, it was no surprise that Kay went on to become a missionary in Asia, where now for more than thirty years God has used her to do damage to Satan's kingdom. She became the pastor of two churches and has had the opportunity to share the Gospel daily on television in her nation.

The Name of Jesus

We have already established that our conflict is with an invisible enemy and his evil agents in the spiritual realm that operate through individuals. We cannot use physical artillery against such enemies, but God has given us invisible spiritual weapons. In fact, they truly are weapons of mass destruction!

In the purse-snatching incident, Kay used one of those primary weapons: the name of Jesus. To unbelievers all over the world, Jesus' name is a common curse word—though you never hear the name of any false religion's founder used as a curse word. Surely this is because all false religions come from the same source: Satan.

For you to use the name of Jesus with authority, of course you must be in right relationship with Him. Consider these Scriptures:

You are my King and my God. . . . Through you we push back our enemies; through your name we trample our foes.

Psalm 44:4–5

The seventy-two returned with joy and said, "Lord, even the demons submit to us in your name." He replied, ". . . I have given you authority to trample on snakes and scorpions and to overcome all the power of the enemy; nothing will harm you."

Luke 10:17–19

They triumphed over him [Satan] by the blood of the Lamb and by the word of their testimony.

Revelation 12:11

One way to use the name of Jesus as a weapon is to speak directly to the enemy, just as Jesus did in the wilderness when He said to the devil, "It is written . . . ," and then quoted Scripture (see Luke 4:4, 8, 12). As Paul Billheimer notes, we should not feel reticent about speaking to the evil powers of darkness:

Many believers have been so tyrannized and dominated by Satan and the prevailing theology of Satan's power and invincibility that, like me, they would never dare to speak directly to him, even in the name of Jesus. For years, I couldn't imagine Satan running away. . . . When I mustered enough courage to speak directly to him in the name of Jesus, it was a great surprise to me to discover an immediate sense of deliverance—as though he had vanished, melted away. . . .

The only way we can be sure that he knows we are resisting him is to *speak aloud*, to directly and audibly confront him with the truth.

May I remind you again that *our resistance* by itself is not what causes Satan to flee; he flees because of the *power of Jesus* which is ours through prayer.[1]

Bible teacher Dean Sherman expands on this thought:

Man . . . has authority; based on what Christ did on the Cross and through His resurrection. Man can still employ Satan through selfishness and sin, but the balance of power on the earth rests with man in the name of Jesus Christ. The authority is complete in man as long as man is in relationship with God through Jesus Christ. With our authority comes the responsibility to use it for God's purposes. If we don't rebuke the devil, he will not be rebuked. If we don't drive him back, he will not leave. It is up to us. Satan knows of our authority, but hopes we will stay ignorant.

We must be as convinced of our authority as the devil is.[2]

When Jesus told His followers, "I have given you authority . . . to overcome all the power of the enemy" (Luke 10:19), He was giving believers the right to exercise power in His name over Satan—God's enemy and ours. We have the right to use Jesus' authority and name to verbally rebuke Satan and his cohorts' tactics.

The Blood of Jesus

The sacrificial death, burial and resurrection of Jesus are the basis of our victory over Satan. In order to redeem us, Jesus had to come to earth in human form, as Hebrews declares: "Since the children have flesh and blood, he too shared in their humanity so that by his death he might break the power of him who holds the power of death—that is, the devil—and free those who all their lives were held in slavery by their fear of death" (Hebrews 2:14–15).

When we confess our sins and repent—meaning, turn from sin—the blood of Jesus cleanses us and puts us in right relationship with God. We call it being born again. Once we have this experience, we are not only protected by the blood of Jesus, but we are also authorized to use the blood as a weapon of warfare.

H. A. Maxwell Whyte says:

> The destroyer cannot get in under the bloodline where it has been placed. But, unfortunately, too many have been loosely taught that Satan cannot ever get through the bloodline. They have not been informed that Satan can and does get through if the bloodline is let down. And how do we let it down? By our disobedience.
>
> We can hardly claim to be under the blood of Jesus if we are walking in deliberate disobedience. . . . Sprinkling or pleading the blood of Jesus without obedience to the Word of God will avail us nothing.[3]

To plead the blood of Jesus means to appropriate our Savior's shed blood as protection from the evil one. This practice is based on the Passover, when the blood of a lamb was applied to the doorposts and lintel of every Jewish home, protecting the inhabitants from the death angel who would pass through Egypt and take the oldest male of every family. The angel passed over those homes that were under the blood (see Exodus 12:1–13).

Of course, the blood of lambs and other animals was a temporary solution for sin. Only the shedding and appropriating of the blood of Jesus provided a permanent atonement. Whyte writes:

> In the natural world, we would have no difficulty understanding how to apply disinfectant to an infection. We would take the disinfectant and sprinkle or pour it upon the infection, and the

result would be that all germs and living organisms present in that infection would die.

Now, we should have no difficulty in doing the same thing spiritually. Wherever Satan is at work, we must apply the only corrective antidote there is—the blood of Jesus. There is absolutely no alternative, no substitute. Prayer, praise, worship, and devotion all have their part in our approach to God, but the blood of Jesus is the only effective counteragent to corruption.

This is why Satan has always tried to take the blood out of our churches. If there is no disinfectant, then his demons are free to continue their deadly work of destruction in spirit, soul, and body.[4]

In any situation where you sense you are in danger or under satanic attack, that is the time to plead the blood and declare its power over the evil one. By so doing, you remind God that you are trusting in His mercy; you also remind Satan that his power is null and void as long as you are under the blood of Jesus, and you remind yourself of the reason for your confidence in Christ.

I (Ruthanne) learned in a dramatic way the power of the blood of Jesus as a weapon. Years ago, my husband, John, went on a mission outreach to Haiti with a group of his students. One Sunday afternoon, he joined two other missionaries to drive to a remote village church up a mountain outside Port-au-Prince. To get there, they left the main road, drove on a small "goat track" road and then parked the jeep and walked the rest of the way.

As John drove on the return trip, he inched up the small road to reach the main road but was unable to see over the nose of the jeep because of the incline. Suddenly he realized that the right front wheel had gone off the road. The missionary in the front seat immediately cried out, "The blood of Jesus! The blood of Jesus! The blood of Jesus!"

By all the laws of physics, the jeep should have crashed to the valley several hundred feet below. Instead, it surged upward, spanned a gap between the road and a boulder, and stopped. The front differential rested on a rock on the other side of the gap; the left rear wheel was the only wheel on solid ground.

John and the missionaries climbed out of the jeep on the uphill side and had a thanksgiving service in the middle of the road. At that moment, the pastor John had preached for that morning drove up in his small truck. "I was praying for you and had a feeling I needed to come check on you," he said. A group of students were with him, and they helped maneuver the jeep onto the main road so they could tow it down the mountain.

As they drove on, they came upon a group of men carrying a Haitian's body from a ravine below up to the roadside. He had been killed when his car had gone off the road about the same time as John's near brush with death.

"It seemed a malevolent spirit was determined to kill someone on that road, and he took revenge on a person with no divine protection," John reported.

He continued, "After I returned to Dallas, an intercessor friend told me the Holy Spirit had given her and a group of students a burden to pray for my safety on that trip. They had prayed fervently two weeks before I had even left; the Holy Spirit showed her that the devil would try to kill me in Haiti. Later a missionary friend told me the road has a voodoo curse on it, and a certain number of people are killed on it every year. Thank God for obedient intercessors, the power of prayer and the protection of the blood of Jesus!"

Arthur Mathews declares, "The only man [or woman] who can keep the enemy at bay is the intercessor, and blessed is that intercessor who knows how to use the power of the blood in spiritual warfare."[5]

The Power of Praise

> Jehoshaphat appointed men to sing to the LORD and to praise him for the splendor of his holiness as they went out at the head of the army. . . . As they began to sing and praise, the LORD set ambushes against the men . . . who were invading Judah, and they were defeated.
>
> 2 Chronicles 20:21, 22

In the passage above that recounts a victory for the people of Judah, men were given a special assignment to go before the opposing army and sing praises to God for His mercy— truly an unconventional strategy of warfare! Additionally, it was after the people had fasted and prayed in unity that God spoke through a prophet to give the leaders His battle plan (see verses 3–4, 14–17). Instead of focusing on the power of their enemies, they praised God in advance, and God sent ambushes to wipe out the coalition of three enemy armies. This victory was so spectacular that Jehoshaphat and his men spent three days collecting spoils from the dead soldiers, which included an abundance of valuables (see verses 24–25).

No matter how fierce the attack may be, we would be wise to follow Jehoshaphat's example: to sing and declare praises to God *before* seeing the victory.

Praise has a threefold purpose in spiritual warfare:

1. It glorifies God and keeps our focus on Him and His power.
2. It terrifies the enemy and throws his ranks into confusion.
3. It encourages the believer as he or she proclaims the victory in the spiritual realm before it is manifested in the natural realm.

Walking in a spirit of praise helps us remember that we fight from a position of victory, not defeat (see Ephesians 1:18–23). Often circumstances look totally bleak just as we are on the threshold of a breakthrough because the enemy hurls his worst shot just before his defeat is sealed. Therefore, it is always too soon to quit!

Scripture says that "[God's] way is in the whirlwind and the storm, and clouds are the dust of his feet" (Nahum 1:3). Arthur Mathews reminds us, "Nowhere is the greatness of God seen to such advantage as it is in His ability to use as His chariot of conquest the circumstances that pose the greatest threat to His cause."[6]

The next time you find yourself threatened by dark clouds and a whirlwind, remember that God rides above the storm to see His purposes fulfilled. Lift up praises in advance, thanking God that you can trust Him to bring you through the darkest storm.

The Power of Voice and Action

Our mouths are our most effective means of using our spiritual weapons. God says His word will not return void (see Isaiah 55:11), so I (Quin) use my voice to praise Him, to declare His Word and to war against demonic power.

I sometimes shout before I have even seen any signs of victory, just as the Israelites did before the walls of Jericho collapsed (see Joshua 6:1–21). God's battle plan called for them to march for six days in silence and on the seventh day to shout aloud at the sound of the trumpet. We may need to raise such a battle cry, or shout, too, as these verses indicate:

> Clap your hands, all you nations; shout to God with cries of joy.
>
> Psalm 47:1

> Sing, O daughter of Zion! Shout, O Israel! Be glad and rejoice with all your heart, O daughter of Jerusalem! The LORD has . . . cast out your enemy.
>
> Zephaniah 3:14–15 NKJV

We can also use our mouths to laugh. *Laugh* in the biblical sense includes the meanings "to mock, to play, to make sport, to deride, to laugh, to scorn." There is also a laugh that is merry, and it does our hearts good like a medicine (see Proverbs 17:22). David wrote, "When the LORD restored the fortunes of Zion . . . our mouths were filled with laughter, our tongues with songs of joy" (Psalm 126:1–2).

Examples of women in the Bible who rejoiced are Miriam (see Exodus 15:20–21), Hannah (see 1 Samuel 2:1–10) and Mary (see Luke 1:46–55). And Paul wrote, "Rejoice in the Lord always. I will say it again: Rejoice!" (Philippians 4:4).

We see the power of laughter in Anne, a young Bible-school graduate who felt God's call to go on an African mission outreach but had no money for the trip. When she and her prayer partner prayed, the friend saw a vision of two bags falling at Anne's feet with the needed two thousand dollars. Uncontrollable laughter hit Anne.

"I am going to laugh my way to Africa," she told her praying friend.

In just two days, all the money came in through unexpected ways.

"I laughed at the devil while I was waiting for the money," she said, "because I knew he wasn't going to keep me from going on God's mission. I also laughed with joy over what God was going to accomplish."

Anne has since served the Lord in several nations, depending entirely on His provision. In Southeast Asia, she has coordinated prayer for her nation by teaching and mobilizing prayer groups from many churches and denominations. She is still laughing at the enemy!

It is not just our mouths that carry power, though. Our bodies do, too. David wrote, "Praise be to the LORD my Rock, who trains my hands for war, my fingers for battle" (Psalm 144:1). I often use my hands in warfare intercession. When I did a word study on the hand, I discovered many Scriptures related to God's hand and warfare:

> Your right hand, LORD, was majestic in power. Your right hand, LORD, shattered the enemy.
>
> Exodus 15:6

> His right hand and His holy arm have gained Him the victory.
>
> Psalm 98:1 NKJV

> For I am the LORD your God who takes hold of your right hand and says to you, Do not fear; I will help you.
>
> Isaiah 41:13

One form of the Hebrew word for *hand* means "open hand," while another form means "closed hand." In prayer, I extend my open hand to the Lord, beseeching Him on behalf of the person for whom I am interceding. In warfare, I close my other hand into a fist and shake it at Satan, declaring the Word of God on behalf of the one for whom I am battling.

I also clap my hands loudly. I see two reasons for this in the Bible: to praise the Lord and to mock God's enemy (see Psalm 47:1–2; Lamentations 2:15). The Scriptures say:

> This is what the Sovereign LORD says: Strike your hands together and stamp your feet and cry out "Alas!" because of all the wicked and detestable practices of the house of Israel.
>
> Ezekiel 6:11

> "So then, son of man, prophesy and strike your hands together. Let the sword strike twice, even three times."
>
> Ezekiel 21:14

Striking my hands together, then, I may say, "You spirit of discouragement, be gone! You have no place in this home, which is dedicated to the Lord God of hosts." Still clapping, I applaud the Lord, saying, "Thank You, Lord, for Your spirit of peace. I applaud You, for You are on the throne as king of my life and my home. Nothing is impossible for You, Lord!"

One intercessor uses her tambourine in spiritual warfare, symbolically striking the enemy as she strikes the instrument with her hand. God gave us a body and creative ways to praise Him with it—as well as ways to use it in warfare against His enemy—so our prayer times need not be dull!

The Importance of Strategy

Paul warned the early Christians to stand against the devil's "wiles," or strategies (Ephesians 6:11 NKJV). Strategy is the science and art of conducting a military campaign on a broad scale. A military commander sets the goal for the campaign and then devises methods for achieving it. Tactics are the specific methods he or she employs to fulfill the strategy, based upon reports from intelligence agents and surveillance equipment.

If the devil has schemes, or military strategies, then we certainly need God's strategy for the specific battles He calls us to fight. The Holy Spirit is the intelligence agent who knows the enemy's strategy and tactics; it is critical that we seek His guidance and fight our battles accordingly.

As a young Christian, I (Quin) thought I could fight every giant, pray for every troubled marriage and intercede for any problem I saw. But I soon learned that not every battle is mine to fight and not every battle strategy is the same. We cannot standardize spiritual warfare, as Scripture makes clear.

We see many different battle plans in Scripture. David learned to inquire of the Lord, "Shall I go to battle?" Sometimes the

Lord would say yes, and sometimes He would give different instructions. Once He told David to wait until he heard "the sound of marching in the tops of the mulberry trees" (2 Samuel 5:24 NKJV)!

When I am seeking God's guidance for a strategy, I use what I call a Four-W strategy. The four Ws stand for *worship, wait, Word* and *warfare*. I *worship* the Lord. Then I *wait* in His presence until He quickens something in His *Word* to use in *warfare* against the enemy in the battle at hand.

I don't necessarily need to do warfare every day, but when I do, my "quiet time" is not always quiet. I may speak loudly, stamp my feet, laugh and/or clap. At other times I may be very quiet, praying to the Lord with hands uplifted or by bowing, kneeling or lying prostrate on the floor while seeking His intervention.

The Strategy of Agreement

Jesus said, "If two of you on earth agree about anything they ask for, it will be done for them by my Father in heaven. For where two or three gather in my name, there am I with them" (Matthew 18:19–20). The prayer of agreement is a powerful strategy in spiritual warfare.

The word *agree* in Matthew 18:19 is based on a Greek root from which we get our English word *symphony*. It means "to be in harmony or accord concerning a matter." We believe it is essential to have at least one specific friend—someone familiar with the current battles we are dealing with—to stand in agreement with us as prayer support in this harmonious way. Such partners also provide a blanket of prayer for us when we are traveling, ministering—or writing a book!

Prayer partners play a spiritual role that is analogous to the army specialists who create a corridor of safety for tanks and other armaments to be used to mount an offensive against the enemy. These soldiers detonate land mines and IEDs (improvised explosive devices), bulldoze man-made barriers and build emergency bridges so that the army can invade enemy territory. Prayer partners often pray in advance to help neutralize the enemy's influence in a given region where workers are planning to declare the Gospel in territory that is hostile to Christianity.

Individual prayer and warfare is important, but interceding with a prayer partner or a group of believers strengthens the prayer's effectiveness. There is strength in numbers. If the two of you or the entire group is in unity, the warfare is even stronger—fasting together makes it stronger still.

Over the years, both of us have experienced the joy of personal prayer partners. I (Quin) prayed with my friend Lib for five minutes on the phone on weekday mornings for seventeen years. We prayed specifically for our families. Wherever I moved, I enlisted at least one woman intercessor to meet with me regularly. Now I exchange prayer requests with about ten friends via phone, email or text.

I (Ruthanne) have a few prayer partners with whom I have been praying for more than thirty years—women of like mind and spirit who can be trusted with confidential prayer needs. Plus, I have a larger group with whom I stay connected via email less frequently. These are friends I can depend on for prayer support when I am under attack. My husband used to call them my "prayer posse," knowing he was often the beneficiary of their prayers.

To pray in agreement, we first ask the Lord *how* He wants us to pray. Then, in agreement, *with one mind*, we pray as He directs, persisting with our prayer partners until we see results. According to Romans 8:26–27, the Holy Spirit can pray through us in accordance with the will of God. So when we pray in this manner, we are praying in agreement with the Father's will.

The Strategy of Nonjudgment

Jesus Himself warned, "Do not judge, or you too will be judged. For in the same way you judge others, you will be judged" (Matthew 7:1–2).

Consider the prayer strategy Lillie learned about judging her brother-in-law. She cringed whenever she heard Robert berate her younger sister, and she and her siblings often judged and criticized him to one another.

One day the Lord convicted Lillie, saying, *If you spent as much time praying for him as you do judging and criticizing him, I could have done more in his life by now.* Immediately, she recognized her sin of judging and asked God's forgiveness. Then she called her family members together, explained the need not to judge, and led them in prayer for Robert. They all agreed to continue praying regularly that he would accept Jesus as Lord and have a change of heart.

Three years later, following a heart attack and open-heart surgery, doctors offered little hope for Robert's recovery. After three weeks in a coma he woke up, but when he opened his eyes he could not see. He was blind.

Yet something miraculous had happened. Sometime while in his coma, Robert had an encounter with the Lord. Now, instead of lashing out, he told his wife, "I saw the Lord and I have a lot to make right."

When he was moved to a hospital bed at home, people noticed he was smiling, not complaining. He was now a grateful, caring, compassionate man; belligerence was no longer on his tongue. God had indeed changed his heart in response to his family's earnest prayers. As his wife's pastor made regular visits to his bedside, praying and reading Scripture to him, they became good friends.

"He went into surgery with physical eyes and then lost his eyesight, but he came out with spiritual vision," Lillie says.

"He also had a spiritual heart healing, even though his physical heart was not permanently healed."

Lillie is confident that their learning to pray without judging was the key to seeing their prayers answered for Robert's salvation. When he died a few months later, they were indeed grateful they had obeyed the Lord.[7]

The Strategy of Binding and Loosing

Another strategy in our spiritual arsenal is binding and loosing. Jesus gave us His authority over the devil and his cohorts, but to see results we must be motivated to use that authority. Consider what He taught His followers: "I will give you the keys of the kingdom of heaven; whatever you bind on earth will be bound in heaven, and whatever you loose on earth will be loosed in heaven" (Matthew 16:19). He also said, "No one can enter a strong man's house and plunder his goods, unless he first binds the strong man. And then he will plunder his house" (Mark 3:27 NKJV).

To bind evil spirits means to restrain their movement by addressing them directly and forbidding them to continue their destructive activity. Through the power of the Holy Spirit, our words loose the person from the enemy's bondage. In prayer, we ask the Holy Spirit to minister to the person's need. Our prayer is directed to God, our warfare at the enemy. This tactic of binding evil spirits is especially effective when praying in agreement with a prayer partner.

Sharon learned to use this important tactic one day when she went to visit her nineteen-year-old son. Not finding him at home, she went on in and was shocked at the mess she found. She thoroughly cleaned the apartment, cooked a meal and then washed all the dirty clothes lying around.

While putting things in order, she found a gun Mike had stolen from his stepfather. It had one bullet in it. Realizing that

Mike was possibly planning to harm himself, Sharon began to do spiritual battle for her son's life.

"Thank You, Lord," she prayed, "for giving us authority to use Your name to set captives free! I plead the blood of Jesus over Mike and ask You to protect his life."

Then, addressing the enemy, she declared, "I come against the strong man of suicide operating against my son and bind your power in Jesus' name. I bind all spirits of rejection, hate, anger, murder and self-destruction, in Jesus' name. I bind all unclean spirits associated with drug abuse, and I cut Mike loose from past hurts and unhealthy relationships. I command the spirits that are blinding and controlling him to release him, in Jesus' name."

She finished by praying, "Lord, let Your peace permeate this apartment. Show Mike how much You love him and desire to set him free from the bondage of the enemy. Thank You, Lord, for protecting his life and drawing him into fellowship with You."

Sharon sang and filled the place with praises to God as she cooked and cleaned. Before leaving, she posted a note: *Mike—I did this today because I love you. No strings attached. Mom.*

Several difficult years passed before Mike finally came to Sharon and asked her to pray for his deliverance, but at last he was set free.

"If I hadn't fought for Mike and kept showing him unconditional love," Sharon said, "I don't think my son would still be alive. But he is alive, and he's serving the Lord with his wife and children."

In some cases, the strong man that needs binding is readily discerned; at other times it is less obvious. We must depend on the Holy Spirit in every situation to reveal the appropriate strategy and empower us to get the job done.

In other cases, that means asking the Lord to reveal how we, or someone we are praying for, has opened a door to an attack. In the next chapter, we will look at the things that give the enemy access to us.

Prayer

Thank You, Father, for the spiritual weapons You provide and the wisdom You give for using them effectively. Help me always to depend upon Your strength in every battle and never to lean on my own understanding. Lord, I want to be a spiritual warrior who remains faithful until victory comes and You receive the honor and glory. In Jesus' name, Amen.

7

An Open Door to the Enemy

You shall have no other gods before or besides Me. You shall not make yourself any graven image. . . . You shall not bow down yourself to them or serve them; for I the Lord your God am a jealous God, visiting the iniquity of the fathers upon the children to the third and fourth generation of those who hate Me, but showing mercy and steadfast love to a thousand generations of those who love Me and keep My commandments.

Exodus 20:3–6 AMPC

Pauline was a compulsive buyer, addicted to shopping. She had credit cards for most major department stores in Atlanta and used one nearly every time she went into a store. She could not resist buying something—clothes, knickknacks, appliances, furniture, gifts. For Pauline, shopping was more than a hobby. It took precedence over other priorities—it became an idol. "It's how I got my kicks," she says.

When Pauline heard a Christian teacher speak on family generational weaknesses, she suddenly realized that her father was addicted to alcohol, but she and her sister were obsessive shoppers. It was a different "substance" but the same compulsive behavior pattern.

Following the teacher's suggestions, Pauline confessed her sin and asked the Lord to forgive her. Then, to break the habit's control over her, she declared aloud: "Satan, you will no longer have a foothold in my life by making me greedy for things I don't need. I renounce this idol and declare the stronghold broken by the authority of Jesus Christ. I recognize this bondage of generational weakness, and by the blood of Jesus I sever it."

Then she prayed, "Heavenly Father, I yield to You in this area, trusting You that this bondage is removed from my life. Thank You that by the power of the Holy Spirit and according to Your Word, I can and will walk in victory and obedience to You. I make You, and You only, the Lord of my life. In Jesus' name, Amen."

Besides having counseling sessions with her husband and their pastor, Pauline destroyed all of her credit cards as an outward sign that she would walk in her deliverance and keep her focus on Jesus.

Our Spiritual Heritage

What is the origin of such a compulsive-addictive behavior? What about other problems, such as uncontrollable anger, adultery, fear of crowds, rebellion or chronic illness? How is it that the enemy has access to us as Christians?

Unfortunately, there is no pat answer, for various factors are involved in such problems. But according to Exodus 20:3–6, we can find one of these factors in our family tree. God says that the serious sin of idolatry will have repercussions upon future generations. Just as our genetic heritage determines what our physical characteristics will be, so our spiritual heritage bears strongly on our behavioral tendencies, both positive and negative.

The iniquity of our forefathers brings a curse upon the family line, opening a door to the enemy. This word *iniquity* does not mean individual sinful acts; it means "perverseness" and comes from a Hebrew root meaning "to be bent or crooked."[1] The word implies a basic attitude of rebellion plus the consequences that iniquity produces. We see the same word in the prophecy concerning Jesus the Messiah: "The LORD has laid on him the *iniquity* of us all" (Isaiah 53:6, emphasis added). Jesus bore the cumulative sinfulness of humankind.

We are not accountable for our forefathers' individual acts of sin; we have plenty of our own for which we are responsible. And Galatians 3:13 declares that Jesus became "a curse for us," providing a means for our deliverance. But we do inherit a susceptibility to sin in the same areas that troubled our forefathers. We tend to be bent, or crooked (weak), in the same places—as Pauline's case illustrates. Our enemy is not omniscient, but he knows where these weak areas are because his agents have been working against our family members and all humankind for generations.

We see such sin patterns in families all the time, including those in the Bible. Look at Abraham, the patriarch we laud as a godly example. On two occasions he lied about his wife, Sarah, calling her his sister. Then Abraham's son Isaac lied about his wife, Rebekah, saying she was his sister. Isaac's son Jacob deceived him so that he could receive the blessing due the firstborn, Esau. Then Jacob's sons deceived him about his favored son, Joseph, causing him to grieve for years. The tendency to lie and deceive showed up in succeeding generations, each time causing more serious consequences.

King David's besetting sin was his adultery with Bathsheba. Although he repented, his infant child died, and sexual sin also became a problem with his other sons. Finally, because his son Solomon took hundreds of foreign wives and began to worship their false gods, God took the kingdom from him. The gravity of Solomon's sin was even greater than that of his father, David.

Sins That Bring Curses

We read in Deuteronomy 27–28 that curses are promised in return for these six sins: idolatry, dishonoring of parents, dishonesty and deception, cruelty to the helpless, sexual sin of any kind and disregard for the law.[2]

Pastor Burton Stokes writes:

> There is that unseen and mysterious connection between a father's sins and the path of his children. If the father commits certain kinds of sin, his offspring are prone to the same kinds of sin, regardless of their training, or the social, cultural, and environmental influences on them. . . . Sin is committed and iniquity is "passed down" to the children, to the third and fourth generation. . . . Each generation adds to the cumulative iniquity; further weakening the resistance of the next generation.[3]

We do not mean to imply there is any deficiency in the power of the blood of Jesus, which redeems us from the curse of sin, or that believers today are bound to the letter of Old Testament law. But if we rebel in our hearts and create idols in our lives, we can be ensnared again by the same yoke of bondage from which we have been delivered (see Galatians 5:1, 16). Thus, we again become susceptible to the curse.

Bible teacher Derek Prince writes:

> Sometimes curses may not have their origin in previous generations. They may be the result of deeds or events in your own

lifetime. Or it may be that a curse from previous generations has been compounded by things you yourself have done. . . . Christians who are undisciplined, disobedient, and out of harmony forfeit their claim on God's protection.[4]

These insights are not intended to bring us into fear or bondage, or cause us to attribute every problem, habit or bad character trait to a curse or a demon. Emotional and behavioral problems sometimes have a physiological or biological basis. For instance, food allergies, PMS (premenstrual syndrome) or menopause may cause such symptoms as depression, anxiety, irritability, headaches, dizziness, mood swings and more. Of course, prayer is always appropriate, but such problems may also call for diet modification, hormone supplements or vitamin therapy. We recommend asking the Lord for guidance in these matters, and if He so directs, consult a doctor.

Looking at the various factors involved with behavior problems helps us become aware of our vulnerabilities. Then we can renounce the sins to which we have yielded in our weak areas and, with the help of the Holy Spirit, strengthen our defenses against the evil one.

The Danger of Idolatry

Though God strictly forbade Israel to engage in any form of idol worship, His people rebelled against Him. They committed spiritual adultery as they took up their neighbors' evil ways of idolatry. As a result, God removed His protection, allowing their enemies to capture and enslave them. McCandlish Phillips explains the gravity of this sin:

> Satan lusts for worship. Because it belongs exclusively to God, he desires it for himself. . . . He sets up many objects as alternatives to the worship of God. This is idolatry in the crudest form. . . .

> Satan stands behind every image and every idol, receiving as unto himself the worship, the respect, and adoration that is directed to them, which belongs only to the living God. . . .
>
> . . . The cumulative effect of idols and images is to bring a curse upon the land.[5]

Over the many years I (Ruthanne) traveled overseas with my late husband, I observed that the areas of the world filled with idols and false religions are generally among the poorest and most disease-ridden nations on earth. John and I became more keenly aware of the need for prayer coverage and God's protection when we would travel in those areas. In fact, I began sending my prayer partners details about our itinerary and ministry schedule so they could pray specifically for us—and their prayers helped make a difference on many of our trips.

Once, on a trip to India, our intended host had become ill, so we were guests of a family who were nominal Christians. Hideous images of Hindu gods hung on the walls of our room, but we were too blurry-eyed from jet lag and 36 hours of travel to give them more than a passing glance as we fell into bed. In the middle of the night, fireworks celebrating a Hindu festival awakened us. A sudden wave of nausea swept over me, and my head throbbed with pain. Sensing an evil presence emanating from those images in the room, I began to bind the spirits of bondage, oppression and the Antichrist and to plead the blood of Jesus over myself.

My husband commanded all evil spirits to leave, and then he prayed for my healing. We dedicated that room to God for the week of our visit. For the next five hours, we played tapes of praise and worship music.

After resting and recuperating the next day, I was able to keep my speaking engagement. But the entire time we traveled around India on that trip was a spiritual battle.

I do not believe our host family gave credence to those graven images on the guest-room walls; they probably considered them a part of the room's decor. But the images gave the evil spirits a legal right to be present until we drove them away. In fact, the artisans who make such objects often do their work under demonic influence and invite evil spirits to inhabit the objects. I believe I was vulnerable to attack because of fatigue and because I was not alert and attentive to the Holy Spirit.

We had a similar experience in Bali, Indonesia, a few years later. The boy who cleaned our hotel room every day gave us a carved figure as a gift on the day we left. We accepted it graciously and gave him the customary tip for his services. After arriving at our next stop, John and I both began having physical problems. We suspected these problems had to do with that little statue, and we learned it was the image of a Hindu warrior god. When we got rid of it, we both recovered.

People in Western cultures rarely bow down to images or idols, although the influx into this country of New Age and Eastern religious practices has made it more prevalent in recent years. But many New Testament references to idolatry equate this sin with rebellion, infidelity, immorality and other sins of the flesh (see Romans 1:22–25; Galatians 4:8–9; Colossians 3:5). One commentator writes:

> The modern believer must understand the vicious nature of idolatry. While we may not make or bow down to a statue, we must be constantly on guard that we let nothing come between us and God. As soon as anything does, that thing is an idol. In addition to material objects such as houses, land, and cars, idols can be people, popular heroes, or those whom we love. Objects of worship can even include things like fame, reputation, hobbies, pride, and deeds done in the name of the Lord. Idolatry is a dangerous and deceitful sin.[6]

In today's Western culture, we see addictions of every description becoming idols in people's lives. I (Ruthanne) once prayed with a young woman who shared that while growing up, she was made to feel she must be the perfect example of a minister's daughter in her studies, appearance, behavior and every other aspect of life. Now as a mom herself, she realized she had made an idol of perfectionism and that it was straining her relationship with her children, hindering the effectiveness of her ministry to children in her church and even affecting her health.

After we shared an intense time of prayer, she repented for making this trait, which was rooted in pride, an idol in her life. She renounced its power over her and forgave the members of her family who had modeled this behavior during her childhood. Over time, as she was able to walk in freedom from perfectionism, her relationships with those around her improved, as did her health and quality of life.

Infiltration of the Enemy

Perhaps no other question has generated more debate and disagreement among Christians than this one: Can a Christian have a demon?

We firmly believe that a Christian who is walking in right relationship with God cannot be possessed by a demon, as possession implies ownership or total control, and a Christian belongs to Christ, not the devil. But a believer who compromises with the enemy, falling into willful disobedience and idolatry, removes himself or herself from God's protection. Such an individual certainly can be harassed and manipulated by demonic forces.

Possibly the greatest danger is that he or she is then open to being deceived by the enemy. Dr. Ed Murphy, Bible teacher and former missionary, writes:

> Satan's goal is, through deception, to entice believers to sin or commit any act which quenches the Holy Spirit in their lives

and/or to lessen their effectiveness in glorifying God through both personal conduct and Christian service. His desire is to find any area of our lives to which he can attach himself (Eph. 4:27). Through his demons (Eph. 6:10–12) he seeks to find any *sin handles* which give him the right to influence us into actions of disobedience to God.[7]

Dr. Murphy goes on to suggest three main doors through which demons exert influence over a human being:

> The first door is *at birth*. Some Christians were born demonized. This is often called by different names, such as generational sin, familial sin, demonic transference, demonic inheritance or the law of the inheritance of evil. . . .
>
> The second door to demonize Christians is *through child abuse*, in at least four possible areas—sexual, physical, psychological and spiritual. . . .
>
> The third door . . . is through his or her own *willful sinful actions* in childhood, youth or adulthood. This usually occurs in the realms of sexuality, the occult and destructive interpersonal relationships.
>
> Sin has been the scourge of humanity since the Fall. With sin comes demons. . . . Increased demonic activity and increased sinfulness go together.[8]

To the degree we choose to obey God, allowing the Holy Spirit to renew our mind through God's Word, is the degree to which we can overcome Satan's efforts to ensnare us. Consider Peter, who after hearing Jesus say that He would be killed and then raised on the third day, declared, "Never, Lord! . . . This shall never happen to you!" (Matthew 16:22).

Jesus responded, "Get behind me, Satan! You are a stumbling block to me; you do not have in mind the concerns of God, but merely human concerns" (verse 23).

Peter had walked with the Lord all of His ministry years, yet Jesus implies that Satan was influencing this disciple to focus on what he wanted, not on God's plan. Peter's perspective was both limited and selfish, just as ours often is. We can be thankful that Peter's wish did not prevail!

Then we read of Simon the sorcerer, who became a believer and was baptized under Philip's ministry in Samaria (see Acts 8:5–13). Later, when Peter and other apostles laid hands on the new converts and they received the Holy Spirit, the sorcerer offered to pay the disciples to give him that power. But Peter told him, "Your heart is all wrong in God's sight. . . . For I see that you are in the gall of bitterness and in a bond forged by iniquity" (verses 21, 23 AMPC).

Although Simon had become a Christian, the bond to his occult past had not been broken. Yielding to Satan's influence upon his mind, he sought a way to draw acclaim to himself, as he had done before his conversion (see verses 9–11). It appears he received the rebuke, as he asked Peter to pray for him, but the narrative about him ends there.

And what about Judas? For three years, he associated closely with Jesus almost daily. Yet Satan entered his heart and caused him to betray the Master (see John 13:21–27).

In ministering to hundreds of people all over the world, we have seen countless examples of believers under demonic bondage to one degree or another. Many, until they receive teaching on this subject, are unable even to identify their problem clearly. They just know something is wrong, and they long to be free.

Once after I (Quin) had been teaching a Christian women's group how to pray for their families, a woman asked for prayer.

"If there's anything in me that is blocking prayer—and there must be, because my prayer life is so lacking—I want to be free," she whispered.

I studied the woman's face and noticed a strange stare in her eyes.

"Is Jesus Christ your personal Lord?" I asked.

"Yes, for over ten years," she said, nodding. "I love Him."

The Holy Spirit prompted me to ask, "Do you have a Native American heritage? Or do you think a curse could have been sent against you?"

"My granddaddy was an Indian chief," she answered.

Before I could even begin to pray, the woman spun into an Indian dance, complete with war whoops and shrieks. Having never encountered such a demonic manifestation, I was numb with shock for a few moments. Then several of us gathered around her and began singing about the blood of Jesus.

Taking authority in the name of Jesus, we commanded the evil spirits to be silent. In moments, the woman quieted down and began responding to our prayers. She declared any curses against her to be null and void by the power of Jesus Christ. She asked God's forgiveness for the sins of her forefathers and for her own sin, and she ordered all unclean spirits to depart, never to torment her again.

"I don't know exactly what happened to me tonight, but I feel so free," she said, smiling, after our prayer session. Some of the leaders in the group agreed to follow up and help her walk in her deliverance.

I cannot say whether curses were said over this woman as a child when she was growing up in her Native American family, whether a relative had dedicated her to a false god when she was a baby or whether she herself had opened the door to evil spirits. I can only report what happened that night when she was released from bondage to freely worship the Lord Jesus Christ: Her whole countenance changed before our eyes.

I (Ruthanne) remember hearing the testimony of a woman in Canada who came to Christ from a devout Buddhist background. As her relationship with the Lord deepened, she desired to learn more about prayer and to become an intercessor. But as she prayed to dedicate her life for this purpose, she sensed the Lord saying to her, *You have unclean hands.* As she wept and asked for understanding, the Holy Spirit reminded her of the times she had burned joss sticks and worshiped idols in Buddhist temples. After repenting for the things she had done in ignorance and renouncing her idol worship, she became a strong intercessor. And of course she was effective in helping other people break free from their occult pasts.

Whatever your spiritual history may be, God wants to move you to a higher level of effectiveness in prayer and spiritual warfare. In the process, He can transform what may have been an enemy stronghold or weakness in your life into greater spiritual strength and discernment, enabling you to be a powerful intercessor for others in similar situations.

In other cases, you may be under attack through harassment by an unbelieving boss or fellow employee who has some degree of authority over you. This might occur through verbal abuse, false accusations, a mocking of your faith, unwelcome sexual comments and innuendos, and other bullying tactics.

Some friends of ours who are harassed in these ways use the Word of God to cancel the negative actions or words spoken against them. Binding the enemy, they then declare select verses, substituting personal pronouns to make the verses applicable to their situation. For example, they may adjust Isaiah 54:17 to say, "'No weapon that is formed against [me] will prosper; and every tongue that accuses [me] in judgment [I] will condemn. This is the heritage of the servants of the LORD, and their vindication is from [God],' declares the LORD" (NASB).

Ask God to reveal His strategy to you for combating the harassment attacks. Also, build back your self-worth by reading aloud Scriptures that affirm how much God loves you, His beloved child.

A Mind for Future Generations

Why address this issue of doors being opened to the enemy? To help women overcome generational weaknesses and iniquities, break the cycles of bondage in themselves and in their families, and make their homes a spiritual refuge. Then they can move on to fulfill God's purposes for their lives, become powerful in spiritual warfare and affect future generations.

Consider this story of a woman who chose to put an end to a sin that had run in her family for generations. Abused as a child, Sarah became a promiscuous young woman and got pregnant in her senior year of college. She was not a Christian, but she loved the father of her unborn child, so while her mother urged her to have an abortion, she just could not.

"My grandmother, mother, sister and cousin had all had abortions, and I wanted to break that cycle," she told me (Quin). "I wasn't religious, but something in me longed to do the right thing, and I knew abortion was wrong."

Sarah and the baby's father married, and two days after her graduation their son was born. Eventually they became Christians, and now, three decades later, their family of five is serving the Lord. Sarah even has a ministry for women who have been in bondage as she once was. She also led several family members to the Lord. Sarah believes some godly ancestor in her family line sowed prayers that helped her to choose life over abortion.

"I've been to Germany and traced my family's line back to those who had close ties with Martin Luther and the Reformation—clearly, they were Christians," she said. "But one of my great-great-grandfathers embraced liberalism and had no time for God. The next few generations of my forebears did not acknowledge their Creator, which is why my mom thought nothing of urging me to have an abortion, as she had done. However, I believe the prayers of my ancestors from earlier times were stored up in heaven and released when I needed them."[9]

We read in Revelation 5:8 and 8:3–5 about the prayers of the saints being stored in golden bowls of incense in heaven. Commenting on these verses, Dutch Sheets, in his book *Intercessory Prayer*, explains:

> The Scriptures indicate that our prayers accumulate. There are bowls in heaven in which our prayers are stored. Not one bowl for all of them but "bowls." We don't know how many but I think very likely that each of us has our own bowl in heaven. I don't know if it's literal or symbolic. It doesn't matter. The principle is still the same. God has something in which He stores our prayers for use at the proper time. . . .
>
> According to these verses, either when He knows it is the right time to do something or when enough prayer has accumulated to get the job done, He releases power.[10]

Sarah felt that when she faced a life-or-death choice, God had His angels release the prayers of her ancestors that were in those bowls.

We have the same opportunity—to confess sins and pray for our future generations, believing those prayers are preserved. As we pray for our own family members or when we minister to others, we ask the Holy Spirit to bring to our attention any generational sin or other issues that need to be addressed. We renounce infidelity, divorce, abuse, unforgiveness, addictions, rebellion, occult activity, membership in secret societies and other generational weaknesses as they are revealed. Then we declare that all these doors are closed to the enemy and sealed by the blood of Jesus, and we thank God for His forgiveness and cleansing.

Now that we have learned doors can indeed be opened to the enemy, let's look at how to find these areas and close them.

Prayer

Father, I come before You to confess and repent of my sin and the iniquity of my forefathers. Forgive us for the sins of idolatry, witchcraft, rebellion, immorality of any kind and all addictions [add anything the Holy Spirit prompts you to include]. *By the power and authority of Jesus Christ, I declare that any satanic influence directed toward me or my family was defeated by Jesus' death on the cross and that this family is under the blood of Jesus. I revoke any generational curses and declare they will go no further. Jesus became a curse for us, and we are a generation that serves God.*

Father, forgive us for depending upon any source besides You for peace and fulfillment. Pour out Your supernatural power in my family so that we will not be bound by the things of the natural world. Thank You that my children will take their place in the Body of Christ and fulfill Your calling upon their lives.

Lord, I submit to You, and in the spirit of Psalm 62:5, I declare that my hope and expectations are from You alone. Thank You for freeing us from the bondage of our past and cleansing us by the blood of Christ. Thank You for our positive heritage—for those ancestors who served You and prayed for us. Thank You for releasing Your mercy and blessings upon me and my family. Amen.

8

Breaking Bondages

It is for freedom that Christ has set us free. Stand firm, then, and do not let yourselves be burdened again by a yoke of slavery.

Galatians 5:1

Ellen had been a Christian since childhood, but when things did not go her way, she would verbally attack those who displeased her. She excused her temper by saying, "Well, I'm Irish, and everyone knows the Irish easily fly off the handle."

Ellen's father also had a problem with anger, so that was her particular negative spiritual heritage. It was a vulnerable area where the enemy took advantage, and becoming a Christian did not eradicate her bad temper. She just made excuses for it.

When the Lord spotlighted her problem, Ellen repented, renounced her sins of anger and speaking bitter words, and declared the bondage broken by the blood of Jesus.

"I had to see my anger for what it was—bondage to sin that was rooted in judging and unforgiveness," she said. "I asked the

Holy Spirit to put a guard on my tongue and to alert me when I was in danger of falling into my old habit."

Now Ellen gives attention to walking in an attitude of grace and forgiveness, renewing her mind with Scripture to keep the enemy from ensnaring her again.

Untold numbers of believers struggle with problems similar to Ellen's—or to Pauline's struggle with compulsive shopping, mentioned in the previous chapter—that paralyze their spiritual growth. Such negative behavior is like a chain holding us to an area of weakness from our pre-Christian experience or to a vulnerable area from our negative spiritual heritage. It exists because a door has been opened and we have given the enemy the right to enter.

These bondages typically affect our mind, will and emotions. They influence our thoughts and behavior, resulting in angry reactions, rebellion, depression, compulsive behavior, overeating, lying, stealing, sexual sin, substance addictions and other destructive habits.

The apostle Paul addressed the problem of such bondages when he wrote to the church at Corinth:

> I fear that there may be discord, jealousy, fits of rage, selfish ambition, slander, gossip, arrogance and disorder. I am afraid that when I come again my God will humble me before you, and I will be grieved over many who have sinned earlier and have not repented of the impurity, sexual sin and debauchery in which they have indulged.
>
> 2 Corinthians 12:20–21

Many Christians struggling with these problems are leading defeated lives, burdened with guilt. They try to change their behavior on their own, only to fail and sink deeper into despair. It is only through repenting, forgiving themselves and others and allowing the Holy Spirit to renew their minds that they can be free from the chains that hold them.

Before we discuss how to be free, however, let's first examine some major areas of bondage:

- Generational sin
- Unforgiveness
- Grief and disappointment
- Addictions
- Rejection and a negative self-image
- Illicit sexual activity
- Occult involvement

Because we discussed generational sin in the previous chapter, we will begin by examining the bondage brought about by unforgiveness.

Unforgiveness

Children, in their naïveté, sometimes express profound truth with the simplest of words—or even made-up words. My (Ruthanne's) late husband came home from a weekend preaching trip once and shared part of a version of the Lord's Prayer he had heard from a pastor's young son: "Forgive us our trash-passes, as we forgive those who pass trash against us. . . ."

To *forgive* means "to give up the desire to get even"—or to "pass trash" against someone. It means to renounce anger and resentment, to release one's debtor. It is a decision made with the will, not with our emotions. We can choose to forgive the person who has offended us, whether we feel like it or not.

When we realize that any injustice we have suffered from another person is small compared to our own sin against God, our need to forgive others is put in proper perspective. In other words, the "trash" we have passed against our loving heavenly Father is much worse than all the "trash" others have passed against us!

The Lord's command is clear: "If you forgive other people when they sin against you, your heavenly Father will also forgive you. But if you do not forgive others their sins, your Father will not forgive your sins" (Matthew 6:14–15).

Refusing to forgive a person who offended or hurt you creates an unhealthy bond between you and that person. Clinging to your resentment only increases your bitterness, poisons your relationship with that person and others and makes life miserable. But when you choose to ask for God's help to forgive the aggressor, that bondage is broken. Both parties are released, and the Holy Spirit then can bring healing and restoration. In some cases, a positive bonding in God's love can then take place.

The deeper the wound, the more essential forgiveness becomes, as a woman named Marie discovered. When her parents divorced shortly after her birth, a relative cared for her until her father remarried and brought her into his new home. The stepmother, unable to have children of her own, deeply resented Marie and was cruel to her. As a forlorn little girl, Marie craved affection from her dad, but because of his drive to be successful in business, he was emotionally absent from her life. Marie became promiscuous in her teen years, seeking love and acceptance elsewhere, but soon the pain of repeated rejection made her wish to die.

Then she began attending church with one of her dates because it was the only way his parents would allow him to use the family car. For the first time, she heard the message of salvation in a way she had not understood it before. Over her boyfriend's protests, she stood up and asked Jesus to come into her heart. She wanted assurance of going to heaven.

However, as a result of not being discipled in her faith, Marie soon fell into a worldly lifestyle when she went away to college. Her father got another divorce and remarried, which widened the breach between them. Out of a sense of guilt, Marie felt responsible to take care of her new stepmother, who was an alcoholic and drug addict. In her despair, Marie called some Christians she had known years before and agreed to go to church with them.

That night, she prayed, *Lord, if You will just forgive me, I'll serve You the rest of my life.* As she lifted her hands in worship, she sensed the Lord say to her, *Marie, I've already forgiven you, and I love you.*

Marie dropped out of college, began attending church regularly and, in time, met and married Mike, whose loving, Christian family was everything Marie's family was not. Although Mike's family loved and accepted her, Marie still longed for her own dad and the only mother she had ever known to love her as Mike's family loved him. Trying to ignore the broken area deep inside her, she became active in the church and enjoyed her two children and lovely home. "Yet my pain never went away," she told us.

Then she and her family moved to Central America to work in a training program. Marie determined to serve the Lord there with her whole heart as she immersed herself in the needs of the people, but on the inside she was crying out for wholeness. When someone mailed her a copy of the original edition of this book, she read about the freedom that comes with forgiving.

"I'd always said that I forgave my father and stepmother, but I knew God was telling me to deal with my feelings on a deeper level," she told us. "I realized that without Jesus, my behavior was no better than theirs, and I began to feel real love and empathy for both of them. I truly forgave them as I prayed that God's mercy and compassion would touch and change their lives. I also prayed that God would give my dad a natural affection for me, his only child."

Only three days later, Marie received a letter from her dad that had been written on the same day she had prayed her prayer of forgiveness. The letter had been mailed to a border town and brought to her by one of her co-workers. The note read, "Dear Marie, here's a check. I was thinking about you today . . . thought you might need some money to get home." This didn't seem like much, but to Marie it was huge.

A few months later, Marie went home to try to reach out to her dad. During her visit, the relationship with her father was healed, as she heard words of love and approval from him for the first time in 34 years. "They were greater than gold," she told us. "At last I had received the miracle of my dad's love and his blessing. It was the beginning of a new life for me."

The truth is, we are *required* to forgive if we want to receive God's forgiveness and peace. When we recall Jesus' plea as He hung on the cross—"Father, forgive them, for they do not know what they are doing" (Luke 23:34)—we are faced with our own sin and the need to free others by forgiving them. Gratitude for the mercy God extends to us and a desire to demonstrate that by obeying His Word strengthen us to forgive those who have wounded us.

Grief and Disappointment

Solomon wrote, "Heartache crushes the spirit," and, "A crushed spirit dries up the bones" (Proverbs 15:13; 17:22). Grief is this "crushed spirit" mentioned in Proverbs, and it comes through many causes: a broken relationship; the loss of a loved one, a business, or a job; or broken dreams. It may come through a miscarriage or barrenness or through disappointment in yourself or another person. We can even be disappointed by God, feeling that He let us down when we needed Him.

Victims of grief need to avoid the "If only . . ." treadmill of lamenting their own failure: "If only I'd made my daughter stay at home, that drunk driver wouldn't have killed her. She would be alive today." The enemy uses such tactics to produce in us guilt and despair, which often leads to anger against God.

Grieving should follow a natural process over a reasonable time span. Counselors say this normally ranges from one to three years, although the process of healing may take longer for some. But unresolved, prolonged grief opens the door to spiritual, physical and emotional problems that paralyze spiritual growth.

A young mom at a retreat where I (Ruthanne) was once speaking came for prayer about her uncontrollable anger. "I overreact when my four-year-old daughter misbehaves," she said. "Sometimes I even yell at her for no reason—and it frightens me."

Asking the Lord for guidance as to how to pray, I felt impressed to ask about her family background and her walk with the Lord.

She said her father had died suddenly when she was four years old. In an effort to shield her from grief, her mother and family members never told her how the death occurred, nor did they allow her to attend the funeral. Too bewildered to ask meaningful questions or fathom this loss at age four, she only knew her daddy never came home again.

Over the years, she learned the details of what happened, but her unresolved grief became a deep, bottled-up anger toward God for depriving her of a father in her childhood. When her own daughter reached age four, that anger began boiling to the surface in outbursts against her child and, sometimes, against her husband and even herself.

I assured her that God had not inflicted this tragedy upon her but that in our fallen world, these things happen. Then I encouraged her to release her deep anger over her loss and freely express to God the grief and anguish she had kept buried for so long. As she poured out her heart to the Lord and began weeping, I comforted her as if she were that little girl crying for her daddy.

When her tears subsided, she looked up with a new brightness in her eyes. I urged her to continue opening her heart to the Lord during the remainder of the retreat so He could heal her completely. She returned home feeling as though she had been freed from a bondage she had not even been able to identify.

In order to be free, the grief-stricken person must eventually be able to release her disappointment and say, "God, I don't understand this loss, but I choose to believe that You love me, and I put my trust in You." God can then pour out the "oil of joy instead of mourning" (Isaiah 61:3).

Addictions

Elizabeth goes to the beauty salon four times a week to maintain her impeccable appearance. Betty's addiction is sensual TV soap operas, while Faith's is the neighborhood spa. For Rhoda, keeping a meticulous house takes priority over her husband and children. Martha is a closet alcoholic, and Caroline is hooked on prescription drugs. All these women show signs of addictive behavior.

Webster's says that to be an *addict* means "to devote or surrender oneself to something . . . obsessively." The great danger of addiction is the matter of surrender—allowing the will to become passive. Most addicts insist, "I can stop any time I want to!" But until they become willing to submit to the power of the Holy Spirit to gain release, the chains hold them. Scripture warns, "Abstain from the sensual urges (the evil desires, the passions of the flesh, your lower nature) that wage war against the soul" (1 Peter 2:11 AMPC).

Let's take the example of Caroline. She was in church every Sunday with her husband and two small children, seemingly a model wife and mother. But for ten years, she had been addicted to prescription drugs and wine. She worked as a nurse and had no trouble getting doctors to write prescriptions for her—mainly for weight loss.

"Often when I popped a pill, I'd cry out, *God, help me*," she said. "But I couldn't control myself. I wasn't the mother I needed to be, but I liked the high the drugs gave me, and it was a good escape. I'd follow the pills with wine to help me feel calm."

One day Caroline's sister-in-law came for a visit and shared how she talked to God. *I'd like to talk to God like that too,* Caroline thought. A few days later, she met a missionary who challenged her to ask Jesus to truly become Lord of her life. Although she did ask the Lord to come into her heart, she continued popping pills and drinking. Later, she was shocked to read in the Bible that her body is the temple of the Holy Spirit (see 1 Corinthians 3:16–17).

Lord, if Your Spirit is in me and I am Your temple, I don't want to abuse something so sacred, she prayed. *Please help me stop taking these pills.*

Determined to be set free from drugs, she searched the purses in her closet and got out all the pill bottles she had stashed away. That night she flushed more than a thousand pills down the toilet, never to take another—and she suffered no withdrawal symptoms.

Three weeks later, while sipping wine one evening, she heard a voice say, *That will be the last drink, Caroline.* She looked around and saw no one. Believing it was the Lord, she knew she had to chuck the wine, too. She poured it all down the sink and never craved it again. God's power had broken her bondage!

Caroline has been free of drugs and alcohol for more than thirty years. Best of all, she has a close, personal relationship with Jesus. Today she is a strong intercessor for her family, community and nation.

Addictions—whether to drugs, alcohol, self-gratification, pornography, perfectionism or negativism—usually stem from a desire to escape painful or difficult circumstances. But of course the addiction, which has spiritual roots as well as spiritual consequences, only deepens the problem. Christian psychologist Dr. Archibald Hart writes:

> All addictions have spiritual roots. Human nature is inherently rebellious and selfish. It desires self-aggrandizement and self-satisfaction. Addictions are a direct reflection and outcome of our life of bondage to this rebellion—traditionally called sin. No healing is complete . . . that does not address and remove this bondage. . . .
>
> There are many ways in which addictions can be spiritually destructive. . . . They are forms of spiritual idolatry; they sap energy and demand attention; they create a false barrier between the addict and God; they prevent obedience to God; they perpetuate sin.[1]

Often a person is driven to addictive behavior because of abuses in childhood: rape, rejection, a negative self-image, unforgiveness, guilt or grief. If addictive patterns are in the family line, that susceptibility should be taken into account and dealt with. Ask the Holy Spirit to show you the root cause of the addiction—either your own or of the person with whom you are praying—and seek healing and deliverance in that area.

Such bondage is not always broken as quickly as Caroline's was. Breaking addiction can be a long, hard road as addicts struggle to overcome their compulsions. Christian counseling and support groups are helpful to encourage the person to be truthful and accountable, while providing encouragement and affirmation. Victory comes by persevering in prayer, having a willingness to accept help from others and trusting in God's mercy. If we *will* to be free, we can break the bond of addiction by the power of the blood of Jesus and then live and walk in the Spirit (see Galatians 5:16–26).

Rejection and Negative Self-Image

Words—ours or those of others—have the power to wound or heal the spirit. One survey indicates that it takes at least five positive statements of affirmation to counteract the effects of one negative comment made to an individual. As the Scriptures testify, "The soothing tongue is a tree of life, but a perverse tongue crushes the spirit" (Proverbs 15:4). And again: "The tongue has the power of life and death" (Proverbs 18:21).

I (Quin) once prayed with an attractive woman in her forties who had the mistaken idea she was fat and ugly. She had grown up in a rural area, and whenever her family would drive past a farm with pigs, her mother would teasingly say, "Look at all the little Deenas out there. Watch them eat!"

Wounded by her mother's words, Deena struggled with an image of herself as fat all her life. Together, we revoked and broke that word curse during a time of spiritual warfare and prayer. Then we declared she was God's workmanship created for His glory, and we thanked the Lord that Deena was created in His image. Deena was released from that bondage and is now able to see herself in a new light.

Rosa discovered the power of a word curse when Robert, her fifth grader, came home with a low grade on his semester's work. The teacher had written that she was giving him this grade because he was capable of doing much better.

"When I prayed about it," Rosa told us, "the Lord reminded me of words spoken by my mother-in-law when Robert was six months old. She became angry with my husband when he asked her not to be so hard on her teenage daughter [his younger stepsister]. He hadn't asked her with the right attitude. Reacting angrily, his mother said, 'Wait till Robert's older. You'll find out what it's like not to be able to handle a kid in school!'"

Rosa recalled the Scripture that says, "No weapon forged against you will prevail, and you will refute every tongue that accuses you. This is the heritage of the servants of the LORD" (Isaiah 54:17). Using that passage in her son's situation, she prayed and broke the words his grandmother had spoken over him so many years ago. His grades improved immediately, and soon he was chosen as one of two students in his class to appear on a television program because of his exceptional learning ability. To Rosa, it was confirmation that the word curse was broken.

As children of God, we can make verbal affirmations about our self-worth and dignity by coming into agreement with what His Word says about us: "I am created in God's image" (see Genesis 1:27); "I am fearfully and wonderfully made" (see Psalm 139:14); "Greater is He that is in me than he who is in the world" (see 1 John 4:4); "He will command his angels concerning me, to guard me in all my ways" (see Psalm 91:11). Reflecting on God's thoughts about us helps deflect the negative, untrue words spoken about us or our family members.

Illicit Sexual Activity

Any sexual activity outside the biblical standard for marriage—whether heterosexual, homosexual, child abuse, self-abuse, bestiality or whatever—is sinful, and God's people are continually warned against it. For instance, Paul says:

> Do you not know that he who unites himself with a prostitute is one with her in body? For it is said, "The two will become one flesh." . . . Flee from sexual immorality. . . . Whoever sins sexually, sins against their own body.
>
> 1 Corinthians 6:16, 18

Additionally, the current epidemic of sexually transmitted diseases bears out Paul's warning: "For the wages of sin is death, but the gift of God is eternal life in Christ Jesus our Lord"

(Romans 6:23). Where sexual sin is concerned, the wages can be physical, spiritual and/or emotional death. This type of sin also can open the door to demonic influences.

A victim of incest or rape, though she did not willingly engage in the sexual activity, is nevertheless held by an invisible chain to her aggressor. Because this chain affects her relationship with God and with other people and because it affects her emotions and her self-image, we recommend intensive counseling in such cases—preferably with a Christian counselor who specializes in sexual abuse. This provides her with an opportunity to express her strong emotions and move toward forgiving her aggressor so she can be truly free.[2]

A frequent result of sexual sin is abortion, which has serious spiritual consequences for the women who make this choice.[3] The testimony of an anonymous writer who underwent two abortions—the second one after having become a Christian—supports the claim of such consequences.

Following an abortion at age twenty, this woman, a traditional churchgoer, committed her life to Christ and began studying to become a missionary doctor. While in medical school, she dated a backslidden Christian and became pregnant again. With no support from her boyfriend, and because of a drive to pursue her educational goals, she had a second abortion, which only compounded her problems.

"How ironic it all was," she wrote in an article. "I was willing to lie, cheat and kill in order to 'work for Jesus.' Next to my personal goals, my child's life was not important. Such a selfish agenda almost cost me my life and sanity."

The woman repented and received God's forgiveness, but because she could not forgive herself, the enemy oppressed her with thoughts of suicide.

"Satan oppresses women who choose abortion, bombarding them with guilt, condemnation, remorse, self-justification, self-loathing and suicidal thoughts," she wrote. "These spirits come through the spiritual door the abortion has opened to the enemy—spirits from which the woman must be delivered. A spirit of murder directed inward had a stronghold in my life. I was so oppressed that I could actually hear the demons sing to me: 'Wanna die, wanna die, wanna die!' This went on for many weeks."

The woman's deliverance came when God spoke to her in church through this Scripture: "I will not die but live, and will proclaim what the LORD has done. The LORD has chastened me severely, but he has not given me over to death. Open for me the gates of righteousness; I will enter and give thanks to the LORD" (Psalm 118:17–19).

She realized she had a choice: She did not have to die but could choose life.

The tormenting thoughts of suicide were the devil talking to her. She went home that day prepared for battle. "This is it, devil," she declared to the enemy as she pushed open her front door and walked in. After studying Psalm 118 and Isaiah 38:18–19, she forgave herself and the men in her life who had hurt her.

As she went to bed that night, it was completely dark in her bedroom, with no light coming in from the street. But as soon as she prayed, she saw three rust-colored beings appear on the ceiling.

"I'm going to live and not die, so I can declare the works of the Lord!" she spoke to the demonic beings. "The living will praise him. Death cannot praise the Lord; the grave cannot celebrate Him. I'm going to live—I'm not going to die! Get out, and don't ever come back again, in the name of Jesus!"

When she repeated those last words, the evil beings disappeared.

"Because of God's mercy, I am still alive," she wrote. "Now I am completely free from that spirit of suicide, and I endeavor to live a life that honors the Lord."[4]

Those who have been involved in illicit sexual activities can take these steps:

1. Repent for breaking God's law, and ask His forgiveness for each liaison, naming each one.
2. Declare that all bondages are broken in the name of Jesus.
3. Command all unclean spirits associated with past relationships to leave in the name of Jesus Christ.
4. Decree that the devil has no more right to you in that area because you are under the blood of Jesus.
5. Thank the Lord for His forgiveness and cleansing, and ask for His strength to walk in freedom and not to get entangled again (see Galatians 5:1 NKJV).

Occult Involvement

Deuteronomy 18:9–14 declares that occult activity is an abomination to God. Such activity includes astrology (reading horoscopes), palm reading, Ouija boards, tarot cards, séances, fortune-telling, witchcraft, divination, sorcery, magic, casting spells or hexes, secret societies and more.

A friend of mine (Ruthanne's) shared how she rejected her orthodox Jewish upbringing and "innocently" began reading astrology columns. Soon she acquired her own personal astrologist to give her detailed guidance for decisions, which led to her getting involved in a sect of Hinduism.

"I had declared God dead but was quite open-minded about the occult," Helen said.

In the course of her spiritual pursuits, Helen's congenital lung disorder worsened, and she was hospitalized with severe allergies two thousand miles from home. A Christian couple at the hospital shared the love of Jesus with her and opened their home to her. In the following months, Helen saw her hostess, who had health problems similar to her own, praying and trusting in Scripture until she was healed, while Helen had to return to the hospital, more desperate than ever.

"I needed confirmation that Jesus was real, but I needed it from a non-Christian source," she said.

One of her Jewish friends, who also was into Hinduism, came to visit her after having a dream about praying for her healing. Although the friend's visit came in February, she brought an unusual token—a Christmas card that presented the entire story of Jesus Christ.

Helen's defenses broke when she realized that God had used an unbelieving Jew, now a Hindu, to bring her the message of Jesus. It was a turning point. She allowed a Bible study leader to pray for her healing, then finally acknowledged Jesus as her Messiah. Immediately she was healed of several maladies, and the serious lung problem began improving.

The Bible teacher took Helen through a process of forgiving everyone she had any grievance against and renouncing all her involvement in the occult. After she was baptized in the Holy Spirit, the Lord showed her that her occult past had attracted curses and demons that had to be broken and cast out, and He sent a minister to pray with her to that end. Then she cleansed her apartment by destroying occult books and objects, as the Spirit revealed them to her.

Until she went to be with the Lord more than twenty years later, God used Helen mightily to minister deliverance to many who were caught in a web of deception, as she once had been.

An amazing number of Christians expose themselves to demonic influence by going to a fortune-teller and then saying, "Oh, but I didn't take it seriously." But the truth is, evil spirits *do* take it seriously. Others innocently purchase or accept as gifts items that have occult significance. Such activity, innocent though it may be, opens a door to the enemy, and God's Word speaks strongly against it. God's warning to the Israelites is as appropriate for us today as it was then: "The images of their gods you are to burn in the fire. Do not covet the silver and gold on them, and do not take it for yourselves, or you will be ensnared by it" (Deuteronomy 7:25).

Years ago, I (Quin) did a thorough housecleaning of such objects by going from room to room in my house, asking, "Lord, is there anything here connected with the occult or the demonic realm that is an abomination to You?" I got rid of things I had innocently bought as souvenirs while traveling abroad.

A friend of mine finally got free of depression after she and her prayer partner burned a stack of comic books that her husband had been collecting as a future investment. Satanic and New Age teachings filled their pages, and my friend had had no peace since he had started bringing them home. "When they were gone, my depression lifted, and my husband was glad he'd agreed to let me burn them," she said.

Consider these actions of Paul's converts in Ephesus:

> Many of the believers who had been practicing black magic confessed their deeds and brought their incantation books and charms and burned them at a public bonfire. (Someone estimated the value of the books at $10,000.)
>
> Acts 19:18–19 TLB

Ask the Holy Spirit to reveal to you any literature or objects in your home that are dishonoring to God, and then destroy them and dedicate your home to the Lord.

Walking Free

The bondages described here frequently entangle God's children and render them powerless in spiritual warfare. If the devil cannot get you to renounce your faith altogether, he will try to ensnare you with these traps and make you ineffective. These are steps you can take in order to walk free:

1. Identify the problem. Ask the Holy Spirit to show you any areas of bondage you may have overlooked.

2. Confess and repent before the Lord the sins the Holy Spirit reveals to you.

3. Choose to forgive all who have wounded you; also forgive yourself. Release your anger and disappointment toward God.

4. Receive the Lord's forgiveness and cleansing.

5. Renounce the sin and declare that all doors where the enemy has gained entry are closed and sealed by the blood of Jesus.

6. Ask the Holy Spirit to help you break the thought and behavior patterns you have become accustomed to (see Philippians 4:7–9).

7. Allow the Holy Spirit to daily conform you to the image of Christ.

Walking free from these bondages is important for your own spiritual well-being. But addressing these issues also will increase your effectiveness in fighting for your children, which we discuss in the next chapter.

Prayer

Father, thank You for shining the light of the Holy Spirit into my heart and revealing to me the areas of bondage where I need deliverance. I humble myself before You and confess my sins of rebellion. [Name the areas of sin you wish to confess, speaking out what the Holy Spirit reveals.]

I renounce these sins and declare they will no longer have dominion over me. I close all doors where the enemy has gained entry, and I ask You to seal these areas with the blood of Jesus. Holy Spirit, help me to focus my thoughts on the things of God and break my negative thought patterns and actions.

Father, I forgive [name] *for wounding me; I release him/her from all judgment and ask You to minister to his/her deepest needs. I release my disappointment in You because this happened, and I choose to obey Your Word, which says, "Get rid of all bitterness, rage and anger, brawling and slander, along with every form of malice"* [Ephesians 4:31].

Thank You, Lord, that I am cleansed by the blood of Jesus and called to freedom, not to slavery. I will not be ensnared again with a yoke of bondage [see Galatians 5:1, 13]. *I will walk in my freedom, in the mighty name of Jesus. Amen.*

9

Fight for Your Children

"Don't be afraid of them [your enemies]. Remember the Lord, who is great and awesome, and fight for . . . your sons and your daughters."

Nehemiah 4:14

All her clothing was black, except for a white turtleneck splashed with prints of skulls and crossbones. As she scooted past me to claim her middle seat on our flight to Vancouver, I (Ruthanne) was shocked to see that under her long hair, one side of her head had been shaved. Her jewelry depicted various witchcraft symbols. Pasty-looking makeup, plus heavy eyeliner, mascara, and dark-red lipstick, spoiled her youthful good looks.

She can't be more than sixteen, I thought. *She must be caught up in the witchcraft fad I've read about that's ensnaring so many teenagers.*

The young woman's chatter revealed she was just a typical youngster going to Canada to visit relatives over spring break. "My mom's afraid I'll have trouble going through immigration," she said to the young man in the window seat, nervously brushing her hair to camouflage the shaved area.

Lord, she's so young and naïve, with no idea of the danger she could be getting involved in, I prayed silently. *Father, please reveal Your truth to her. Send someone across her path who can get her attention and witness to her. Give her mom wisdom to know how to deal with this situation.*

Most parents and grandparents realize that today's young people face pressures and temptations that were almost nonexistent when we were growing up. Clearly, the devil has targeted our children for destruction. Like a lioness protecting her cubs from predators, we women need to fight for our children.

A godly mother prays for each child from the moment she cradles her newborn in her arms—often even when the child is still in her womb. And those prayers continue throughout her child's life. Like Jesus' mother, she ponders things in her heart (see Luke 2:19, 51). At every stage of their development, a mother talks often to God about the children He has given to her.

The Battle for Our Offspring

Though many parents seem unaware of it, a battle rages today on many fronts to win the allegiance of our children. Humanist-oriented educators have propagated their philosophy for years through curricular programs in public schools. Initially aimed at neutralizing the basic Judeo-Christian view on which our nation was founded, such programs seek to eradicate these values in order to build a godless, secular state. Some years ago, the late Mel Gabler, a textbook researcher, shared this insight:

> The wording of many texts is designed to first sow seeds of doubt in the student's mind concerning his present values. Gradually he reaches the position of not believing anything;

then the texts subtly indoctrinate the student with new "values," such as anti-Americanism, hatred for the home and family, man as an animal, and anti-Christian attitudes.[1]

Historian David Barton refers to these efforts as *revisionism*, which he defines as "the common method employed by those seeking to subvert American culture and society. . . . [They claim] that the Founders 'reared a national government on a secular basis.'"[2] Even a cursory review of the vast amount of the Founders' original writings shows this claim to be false, yet the trend persists.

According to reports we see in the media and hear firsthand from teachers, students and parents, an alarming number of programs instruct teachers how to introduce students to such ideas as undermining authority figures; demeaning traditional family values; legitimizing witches, casting spells and other aspects of the occult; and affirming themes of despair, hopelessness, manipulation, violence and sexual experimentation. These concepts convey to pliable youth the suggestion that each person can determine for himself or herself a customized worldview that has no foundation in absolute truth.[3]

We also see Satan's influence in the aggressive marketing of commercial toys, video games, cartoons, TV shows, movies, children's literature and secular music. Having been desensitized to the reality of evil in our society, some adolescents unknowingly are connecting with dangerous pedophiles on internet social-networking sites. This is a time for praying parents to be vigilant in cultivating godly values and a Christian worldview in their children.

The Infiltration of New Age

The "do it yourself" sort of religion called New Age—a mixture of Western atheistic humanism and Eastern mysticism—is rapidly replacing our cherished Christian values. There is nothing *new* about it at all, but it is dangerous because its proponents have high on their list of objectives the indoctrination of our children and youth. Former occult practitioner Gregory Reid writes:

> In the last few decades, the New Age has come into full blossom and become part of much of our culture, media and education. If there is a common agenda, it is for One World, one religion, global peace, and realizing man's Divinity. . . . It is tolerant of all faiths, except one—Biblical Christianity. One is free to believe anything one wishes, so long as one does not believe that the Bible is the only truth and the infallible, inspired Word of God and that Jesus is the only way to salvation. . . .
>
> Satan is the father of lies, was a liar from the beginning and still lies, even if he puts on an evangelical suit or a clerical collar. Deception is his most potent weapon. It will be his final weapon.[4]

The risks facing children and youth today may seem too frightening to be real, but they are real indeed. And kids from Christian homes are not immune from these dangers. We, as "watchmen on the wall" (see Isaiah 62:6), need to be aware of Satan's devices and withstand his work through prayer and spiritual warfare. We truly are at war, and the lives of our children are at stake.

Reid also says:

> To fight well you must walk in the power of God. No more ignoring the forces of evil. I challenge you with the words of one teen Satanist girl: "How do you expect me to believe your God has power over the devil if YOU don't believe it?"[5]

Power is the key word here. Power is what occultism is all about, but we women of prayer have a greater power available to us.

The Danger of Rebellion

Because of these shifts in our culture, it is no surprise many parents are dealing with their kids' rebellion against any form of authority. This is the sin that caused Satan to be cast out of heaven and caused Adam and Eve to disobey God's instructions (see Isaiah 14:12–15; Genesis 3:1–6). Scripture declares that "rebellion is like the sin of divination, and arrogance like the evil of idolatry" (1 Samuel 15:23). Our heavenly Father knows the pain that parents feel when their children rebel, only to suffer the inevitable consequences.

Here is how one mom dealt with her son's rebellion.

"Excuse me, son," Hazel said, interrupting Jim, her sixteen-year-old, as he shouted protests about his curfew while she cooked supper. Pointing her finger toward the angry teenager, she said, "Satan, you can't have my son. I bind your activity in him, in the name of Jesus Christ." Then she calmly asked, "Now, Jim, what was that you were saying to me?"

"Oh, Mom, I just forgot," he said, turning to leave the room.

It was the first time Hazel had used her authority as a believer in Jesus to come against the devil's manipulation of or manifestation in one of her children. Though all four of her kids had been reared in a Christian environment, all of them rebelled and chose their own path instead of God's. But about the time Jim's rebellion became a problem, Hazel discovered through her Bible study that the fight was not with her son but with demonic forces that were influencing him. From that point on, her prayers intensified with one goal before her: to see Jim, as well as her older children, turn to the Lord.

It was a long battle. Jim's rebellion persisted, leading him into drugs, crime and a stint in jail, while her older children showed no interest in serving God. For years, this determined mother persisted in prayer and warfare.

One year, all four of her adult children and their spouses came for Christmas, and they agreed to give Hazel one hour of their attention—the only gift she wanted from them. She set up her Sunday school flannel board and took them on a tour through the entire Bible, zeroing in on Christ's sacrifice on the cross for their sins. Captivated by her presentation, the group sat around the dining table for two hours, asking questions.

One by one over the next few months, they all committed their lives to the Lord, and they continue serving Him today. They look back on that Christmas roundtable discussion as a turning point in their lives.

"It wasn't an easy battle," Hazel said. "But I persisted in declaring to Satan that they are God's property and he had to take his hands off them!"

The Value of Vigilance

A single mom named Louisa told me (Ruthanne) how her daughter changed after coming under the influence of a young man she met who was involved in a cult group. Louisa was mystified when her usually obedient child became rude and rebellious and her grades in school fell dramatically. After Louisa and her prayer partner began praying about the problem, her friend called to say, "I feel you need to pray over Kristen's room and ask God to show you whether any occultic objects are there."

Louisa was always careful about what she allowed in her home, so one day while Kristen was at school, Louisa went into Kristen's room. *Father, please show me anything in this room that is not of You that needs to be removed,* she prayed.

Standing quietly and looking around, she saw light reflecting on a shiny object in the pencil holder on the desk—a crystal wand with a glittery cultic image attached to the top of it, which the young man had given Kristen. Louisa destroyed the wand, anointed the room and prayed over it, then prayed that Kristen would not detect anything missing.

Within days, Kristen's grades came up and her rebellion vanished, and she never noticed the object was not there. She also lost interest in the sinister young man who had been trying to establish a friendship with her.

Some may feel the wand was nothing to merit serious concern, but Louisa believes her vigilance in destroying it prevented the enemy from getting an inroad into Kristen's life. Today, married and with a daughter of her own, Kristen is learning valuable spiritual lessons from her mom about child-rearing.[6]

All of us, but especially parents, need to be vigilant about these important issues and teach our children the truth of Scripture. A poll by the Barna Group reveals just how essential it is for parents to be responsible for their children's spiritual formation:

> Overall, less than four out of every ten young people (38%) said that churches have made a positive difference in their life. . . . "Parents must take the lead in establishing the centrality of faith experiences and practices for their children. That begins with parents modeling the significance of faith in their lives. It also highlights the importance of families taking the lead in the spiritual development process, rather than expecting or waiting for a church to produce spiritual growth in adolescents," [George Barna said].[7]

One mom dealing with a rebellious son said it well: "I've learned the importance of praying the Word of God over him instead of just 'praying the problem.' I'm confident that he will fulfill the destiny God has for him."[8]

The Scare of Depression and Suicide

Carrie shared with us the prayer battle she fought for her teenage son Matt, who grew increasingly angry and depressed because of conflict with his father, who often criticized him and almost never showed Matt any affection or approval.

"One day as I was in prayer," she said, "the Lord said to me, *Great fear is coming upon you, but you will have victory over it.*"

Carrie didn't know what that meant, but she increased her prayer time, often praying Malachi 4:6, that God would turn her husband's heart toward his son and vice versa.

That fall, when Matt's senior year began, he was depressed because he did not like school, and he was upset that he did not have his own car. Carrie was troubled about his interest in a horror-film character and by a poster he had placed in his room with an alien-monster figure on it. Standing in his room, she would bind the evil spirits that were bringing oppression against her son.

Shortly after school started, a tenth grader in the community committed suicide by driving his car off a cliff. As Matt's depression got worse, he told his father he felt his mind was about to snap. Carrie and her husband prayed in agreement, pleading the blood of Jesus over their son and asking God to protect him from suicide.

One morning, Carrie had a heart-to-heart talk with Matt about his depression and his girlfriend problems; then she shared some Scriptures with him before he left for school. Through the day, she prayed Psalm 3:3 over him and asked God to raise up intercessors to pray for her son. Late that afternoon, when she returned from a shopping errand, she saw Matt as he was leaving for Bible study and choir practice.

"God bless you, son," she said. "Have a good time, and I'll talk to you tonight."

A few hours later, Matt drove his mother's car off a three-hundred-foot cliff in the same area where the other boy had died, only higher up. He had said good-bye to his girlfriend and then driven to the cliff to read his Bible and pray in an attempt to reach God. Feeling there was no response, he started the car motor, rammed the accelerator and drove off the cliff.

As soon as the wheels left the road, Matt realized he had made a horrible mistake. *Jesus, please forgive me*, he prayed, thinking he was going to die. *Take me home!* He blacked out just before the car landed.

A woman living nearby saw what happened and phoned the police as the car crashed on the rocky seashore below.

Matt crawled from the wreckage in shock. Two Christian policemen walked up to him. "God must really love you, son," one of them said, "because He just saved your life." These men had seen four or five other suicide attempts from that cliff; Matt is the only one who survived.

The policemen saw a Coast Guard helicopter overhead and signaled for help. "Who called you?" one officer yelled to the pilot over the noise as they lifted Matt into the chopper.

"No one—I just happened to be in the area," the pilot answered.

Within minutes, Matt was in the trauma unit of a nearby hospital. When his parents arrived, he was conscious and able to talk. What Carrie had spoken over her son that afternoon came true. God *did* bless him—by saving his life. Also, she *did* speak to him that night—and he was alive!

Matt came through the experience miraculously, only needing to wear a back brace for a few months. He received therapy from a Christian psychiatrist, who was mystified as to why Matt had taken such drastic action. Carrie shared with him about the influence of the demonic realm and the prayer covering that had been placed over her son.

In the days following the crash, Carrie cried out to God one day, *Oh, Lord, what was I doing at the exact moment of the crash?*

That makes no difference, He replied. *What made a difference was what you were doing* before *the crash.*

While Matt was in the hospital, Carrie ripped that horrible poster off his bedroom wall, and he never objected. In the years since the crisis, Matt has reconciled with his father and made great progress spiritually. Today he is married with a family of his own.

As a mother, you must be observant and aware of your children's activities and interests. Try to meet their friends. It is important to pray that your children will form godly friendships; also, pray for the friends themselves. Ask the Holy Spirit to show you specific areas you need to address in prayer.

Counselors working with youngsters who struggle with suicidal tendencies or who are drawn to getting involved with the occult suggest being alert to these indicators:

- Extreme mood swings, such as black depression or violent rage
- Nightmares and deep fears
- Withdrawal from and rejection of family; noncommunication
- Frequent absenteeism and lower grades in school
- Interest in occult reading, unwholesome games and horror movies
- Secret friends and reluctance to have you meet them
- Compulsive lying and excessive swearing
- Rebellion
- Interest in heavy-metal music
- Sexual promiscuity

If you suspect your child is involved in or being drawn toward any of these areas, your first recourse is to pray for God's wisdom in handling the situation. Also pray that God will reveal truth to your child and give him or her discernment to recognize the enemy's attempt to destroy their future. It is helpful to pray in agreement with your husband or a prayer partner; do not carry the burden alone. You also can anoint your child's room, praying over it and declaring Scripture verses.

If you discover something questionable, such as a suicide note, occult objects or illegal drugs, ask the Lord to show you how and when to confront your child and whether you should seek professional counseling for them. Timing is important. Do not jump to conclusions or become angry. Give the child an opportunity to explain, and accept what he or she says at face value. Ask the Lord to guide you to a competent Christian counselor and to reveal anything hidden that should be addressed.

The Wisdom of a Mother

When twenty-year-old Anna dropped out of church and began devoting all her time to a girl she had met in college, her adoptive mother, Valerie, went to war using the Word of God. Anna had lost interest in men and begun focusing on women's sports after being deeply hurt by her boyfriend, but when Valerie tried to talk to Anna about her unhealthy relationship with the girl at school, Anna became defensive and belligerent and distanced herself from her parents.

This praying mom recognized that her daughter's new friend was not the enemy but the means Satan was using to try to prevent Anna from fulfilling God's call on her life. Valerie searched her Bible and compiled Scripture-based prayers that she began praying for Anna daily. Some of those prayers paraphrased verses in this way:

> Even the captives of the most mighty and most terrible shall all be freed; for He will fight those who fight us, and He will save our child, Anna.

> See Isaiah 49:25 TLB

Thank You, Lord, that You have hedged up Anna's way with thorns. You have built a wall against her so that she cannot find her paths. She has followed after her lovers, but she shall not overtake them. Lord, You will betroth my daughter to You in stability and in faithfulness, and she will appreciate, give heed to and cherish the Lord.

See Hosea 2:6–7, 19–20 AMPC

The Lord our God teaches Anna what is best for her; He directs her in the way she should go. She pays attention to His commands; her peace is like a river; her righteousness is like the waves of the sea.

See Isaiah 48:17–18

The blood of Jesus purifies Anna from all sin, for He is the atoning sacrifice for her sins.

See 1 John 1:7; 2:2

Some years later, Anna opened up to share her struggles with her mom, admitting her rebellion and wrong attitudes, her need for healing and her desire to be reunited with her family. She moved out of the city, where so many evil influences pulled at her, and found a new job with a Christian boss. She began replacing the negative elements in her life with positive ones as she renewed her commitment to the Lord.

"The battle for Anna was long and fierce, but the experience drew me even closer to my Commanding Officer," Valerie said. "Today my husband and I have a close, loving relationship with our daughter."

In another instance, a woman named Doris pulled a pornographic video out of her thirteen-year-old son's backpack after he came in from visiting his friend one night. She had felt the Lord's warning that Roger had brought something unholy into their home. The next day, after she and her husband had prayed, she told Roger they knew he was not using the small television in his bedroom just to play Nintendo, but also to watch blatant pornography.

He replied, "I need my privacy."

"Privacy is a privilege—when you abuse it, you lose it," she told him. "Your father and I have established the standard of Christ in our home. You live here by that grace."

Later, Doris prayed over Roger's room, anointing the TV set with oil and declaring that no more unrighteousness be released through it. A few days later, it quit with a big puff of smoke.

When Roger continued to act rebellious, Doris enlisted prayer partners to come to her home to pray. She asked them to pray without criticizing or judging Roger, but rather with concern for a son who needed the Savior. Sometimes the women sat on his bed and just sang praises to God.

Realizing they were in a spiritual battle, Doris wrote Scripture verses on paper and placed them around Roger's room—on top of fan blades, under his mattress, in the closet. This was one way she fought the enemy with the Word of God. As many other parents have done, she also stood on the promise in Isaiah 49:24–25, that the Lord would contend with the evil forces influencing Roger and that He would save her son.

Doris and her husband continued showering Roger with love while remaining vigilant in watchful care over him. Though bouts of discouragement would hit, they never gave up battling for his freedom.

Two years later, Roger not only asked for his parents' forgiveness; he also asked them to get him deliverance counseling. Thankfully, he was set free and has served the Lord ever since.[9]

When looking at seemingly impossible circumstances, it is good to remember something our missionary friend Wayne Myers often said: "Don't tell God how big your mountain is— tell your mountain how big your God is!" These two moms knew all too well the power of the enemy's attack against their children. But they also knew God's greater power was with them in the battle and that they were praying according to His will for their troubled kids to receive His love and freedom. So never give up standing in the gap for your children and loved ones.

The Power of Many Prayers

Some years ago, after a group of five women in Lexington, Kentucky, had read my (Quin's) first book, *How to Pray for Your Children*, they met to watch the accompanying video and decide how they could meet to pray regularly for their offspring. Between them, they had about thirty children and grandchildren.

At first, about twenty moms met in local parks to pray for one another's children. When they shared their vision in local churches, home groups and schools, soon several other such groups formed in the area.

Before long, the husbands of the original five asked if they could join in the prayer. Gathering at one couple's home one night a week, the group started off with a covered-dish supper, followed by praise reports. Then they divided into smaller prayer circles to pray for each other's children. At the end, each person took names of children other than their own to pray for during the following week. Prayer requests were kept confidential.

Over the years, I visited the original group of couples, which included seventeen parents, some of whom were single. After the leader, Elizabeth, died and others moved away, they prayed by telephone as needs arose.

Not so long ago, when I was in Lexington to speak at a church seminar, four young women came to introduce themselves to me afterward.

"We want you to know we are the fruit of our parents' prayers," one said. "Our parents were involved in some of those early Pray for Your Children groups. We knew they were praying for us, and we want to thank you for teaching them."

Misty-eyed, I gathered them in a group hug and prayed aloud that they, too, would become praying moms when they had families of their own.

If you are waging a prayer battle for your son or daughter, be assured that God is working in the unseen realm to impact your child's life. As we have seen in the examples in this chapter, if you refuse to allow the enemy or discouraging circumstances to deter you, victory will come. Yes, your warfare prayers do make a difference—and it is always too soon to quit!

Now let's discuss strategies that will help safeguard your marriage against the enemy's attack.

Prayer

Father God, Creator of all things, thank You for the gift of my children. Please dispatch angels to watch over them and protect them in all their ways [Psalm 91:11], and send Christian friends into their lives to help them and to be godly influences. Lord, what an awesome privilege and responsibility to be a parent! Give me the wisdom and discernment I need to know when my children need my prayers or when I need to be an understanding friend to them.

Father, I pray that my children will fulfill Your plan and purpose for their lives. May "the Spirit of wisdom and of understanding, the Spirit of counsel and of might, the Spirit of the knowledge and of the fear of the Lord*" be upon them [Isaiah 11:2]. I release these gifts You have given* *me, Lord, and place my children in Your hands. Thank You that You love them more than I do, that Your plans for them are plans for welfare and peace, not for evil, and that You will give them a future of hope* [Jeremiah 29:11 AMPC]. *Amen.*

10

Fight for Your Marriage

Wives, in the same way submit yourselves to your own husbands so that, if any of them do not believe the word, they may be won over without words by the behavior of their wives, when they see the purity and reverence of your lives.

1 Peter 3:1–2

"My husband, a Bible study leader, is physically attracted to a woman in our church fellowship. Please pray with me for him, Ruthanne," Alicia pleaded after hearing me teach at a Canadian conference.

"When this woman goes to Carl's office for spiritual counsel, he puts everything aside to spend time with her. Yesterday he did it again," she continued, beginning to cry. "He didn't even bother to call and let me know he'd be late coming home. Sometimes I get so angry, I just want to stop fighting for our marriage. He says he's not sexually involved with her, but he's playing with fire and doesn't even realize it. And he's an officer in the group sponsoring this conference!"

It is an all-too-familiar story for a Christian couple whose marriage is under attack. Because of his pride and his carnal nature, the husband enjoys the interest and attention of a woman seeking his advice, yet he is blind to the danger involved. The wife recognizes the peril, but, feeling hurt and rejected, she directs her anger at her husband instead of at Satan, the real enemy. The rift gets wider, and unless prayer and sober counsel prevail, divorce may be the result.

Reports of infidelity in Christian marriages have sent shock waves through the body of Christ in recent years. What is the answer? Is the influence of secular media and our permissive society just too great for Christians to overcome? What can a wife do under these circumstances?

I told Alicia that I felt Satan was using this other woman's attention as a snare to ruin her husband's testimony and his marriage, and I advised her to renounce her hurt and anger and then forgive both of them.

She prayed and forgave Carl and the woman involved. Then we bound the spirits of deception, pride and lust in both of them. We declared in the name of Jesus that all ties of sexual attraction between Carl and this woman, or any other women he had lusted after, were broken. We asked the Holy Spirit to reveal the truth to him, to expose the enemy's snare and to bring Carl to repentance.

"Now that you've released your husband from your judgment, the Holy Spirit is free to work in this situation," I told her. "Don't argue with Carl about it anymore. Just ask the Lord to help you express love to him."

I was astonished by the swift response to our prayer and spiritual warfare. After the meeting that same evening, I saw Alicia in the ladies' room, and she was radiant.

"Ruthanne, I can't believe the change in Carl!" she exclaimed. "The Lord must have dealt with him during the service, because he came down from the platform during the offering and apologized to me for his involvement with that woman and for hurting me. I told him I forgave him. His whole attitude has changed, and I know the Lord will help us work everything out."

This is an example of approaching a marital problem through spiritual warfare. And in this case, it appears that a much more serious problem was avoided.

Extending Mercy

In today's unfettered society, pornography is a growing problem that threatens many Christian marriages.

One woman's husband, Bob, was out of state for several months on a job assignment, and she discovered he had been making phone calls to pornographic 900 numbers and charging them on their credit cards. Besides being angry, Rachel felt rejected, ugly and cheapened. She called Bob and confronted him with what she had found out, flying into an emotional rage as she talked. He cried and said he wanted to come home and talk it over and work things out, but Rachel refused. Then she called an attorney and scheduled an appointment.

"Only then did I settle down and ask the Lord what He wanted me to do," she says. "He showed me that taking my case to a lawyer was not the answer. Then He told me to begin praying for a spirit of understanding. I cancelled the appointment and said, *God, You told me You would be my defense—I'm depending upon You.*"

About this time, Rachel met one of Bob's aunts whom she had not met before and learned from her that Bob had suffered much rejection during his childhood. His mother had married five times while he was growing up, and he often went to this aunt's house to hide when he was afraid of being beaten by a stepfather.

The Lord showed Rachel that Bob had not received affirmation or positive words as a child and that he was now making these calls because he wanted to hear what he thought would boost his self-esteem. Rachel realized that if they did get back together, she would need to speak positive words of life to him.

"As I was still struggling with my own hurt and rejection, God gave me a graphic illustration of the blessing of mercy," she told us. "The year before, I had opened a small business in my home, for which I filed sales-tax receipts with the state each month. Now that the business had been dormant for six months, I assumed I didn't need to send reports.

"One day a man from the state attorney's office came to my door and bluntly told me I could be prosecuted and sent to jail. Shaken, I explained that I simply was unaware that reports had to be filed if no sales were made and that my papers hadn't even been unpacked since our last move. Suddenly his gruff attitude changed. 'Well, I'll have mercy on you this time and take care of these reports for you,' he said.

"After he left, I stretched out on the sofa and cried. I was being bathed in mercy such as I had never experienced before, and I dropped off to sleep. When I woke up, I called Bob and told him I wanted to show him mercy. I was willing to talk things out."

The Lord gave Rachel Scriptures to pray for Bob. She said to God, *Father, I pray that Bob will not set any vile thing before his eyes and that he will have nothing to do with evil* [see Psalm 101:3–4]. *Bob's body is not made for immorality but for the Lord* [see 1 Corinthians 6:13]. *Thank You that he is free in Christ Jesus and he will not be burdened again by a yoke of bondage* [see Galatians 5:1].

Many Scriptures also ministered to Rachel, such as, "When anxiety was great within me, your consolation brought me joy" (Psalm 94:19), and, "When I called, you answered me; you greatly emboldened me" (Psalm 138:3).

When Bob came home, the couple met with their pastor for counseling. Bob repented, and Rachel asked him to forgive her for her bitter words.

"God not only set my husband free, but He also did a lot of changing in me, as He helped me to begin speaking encouragement and life to Bob," she reported. "For any woman facing this problem, I advise her to wait on the Lord before she takes any action. Then she should get counsel from a godly person and get her emotions under control before confronting her husband. We need to be willing to see the whole picture from God's point of view and work toward healing instead of rejection."

Practicing Tough Love

In one marriage poll, *100 percent* of the women interviewed said they considered faithfulness the most essential requirement for a spouse. Physical attraction was listed by only 19 percent of the women (ages 18 to 24) as being essential.[1] Clearly, a woman wants her husband to love her faithfully and exclusively all his days. Yet stark reality reveals that not all will.

Suppose your husband has had one affair after another and seems impervious to your efforts to get him to deal with the issue. What do you do?

"The lure of infidelity is an *addiction* to an individual who has a chink in his moral armor," says Dr. James Dobson, author of *Love Must Be Tough: New Hope for Families in Crisis*.[2] In discussing the cases of three wives he had interviewed who put up with infidelity in their husbands without confronting them, he says:

> While some people are chemically dependent on alcohol or heroin or cocaine, this kind of infidel is hooked on illicit sex. Psychologically, he needs the thrill of the chase, the clandestine meetings, the forbidden fruit, the flattery, the sexual conquest,

the proof of manhood or womanhood, and in some cases, the discovery. . . . What they needed were wives who were committed to the concept that *love must be tough.* . . .

What is required is a course of action—an ultimatum that demands a specific response and results in a consequence.[3]

A woman wrote Dr. Dobson, telling of the trauma she suffered after learning that her adulterous husband, a pastor, was forced to resign and they were asked to vacate the church parsonage. After prayer, the Lord directed her to a wise counselor who assured her this man's affair was not her fault. He also convinced her that despite the difficulty, she must stand up to her husband and give him an ultimatum without backing down. She wrote:

A few months later the crisis came. I gave Milan an ultimatum—either go with the other woman or stay with me. He could not have both of us any longer. I put my hands on his shoulders and looked him straight in the eye and said, "You know you are to blame for what has happened to us. You committed adultery, I didn't." I told him if he loved the other woman more than me, then he should leave. I would accept it. I reminded him that he had a soul and would someday answer to God.

Milan not only broke off the affair, but he later thanked me for having the courage to stick it out with him through this difficult time. It was not easy but we worked it out and our family survived.[4]

A woman confronted with evidence that her husband is having an affair often reacts in one of two extreme ways.

The first is to ignore the evidence (or rationalize it) and go on with life as if nothing has changed. Some men are happy to continue living two lives, and their wives accommodate them. In fact, in many parts of the world, it is quite acceptable for a man to have a mistress on the side. And in some cultures, a man is free to take a second wife and move her into the house. The first wife must either accept it or move out and support herself and her children. I (Ruthanne) have counseled and prayed with countless Christian women in Africa, Asia and Latin America who face these situations.

The other reaction is to confront the husband prematurely out of hurt and anger. This kind of confrontation usually ends in an emotional shouting match, where nothing is resolved but the breach is widened.

The wise woman who suspects her husband is unfaithful should first go to her prayer closet and seek God's direction. Recognize that your husband is not the enemy; nor is the other woman. Satan is using the human weaknesses of all involved to try to destroy your marriage. Ask the Lord to uncover the things being hidden and to guide you, step by step, in addressing the issue. If you have a prayer partner who is able to keep confidences, you may consider asking her to pray with you for guidance and strategy.

Dr. Archibald Hart gives further advice for a woman in this predicament:

> Divorce is not the only answer to an unhappy marriage. I am convinced that the solution to most miserable marriages is to be found in creative counseling, sound marriage guidance, and, if necessary, individual therapy for the marriage partners—as well as in a mutual turning to God for help and healing. . . .
>
> Of adults who are surveyed five years after their divorces, only about a quarter are resilient—managing to cope adequately with their new lives. Half are muddling along, just barely coping. And the final quarter are either failing to recover or looking back with intense longing to the time before their divorces, wishing the divorce had never taken place. Far from taking care of all their problems, for these people divorce has just added a whole set of new ones.[5]

It takes much prayer, wisdom, tough love, forgiveness and often counseling to recover when infidelity occurs in a marriage. The offended spouse struggles with issues of trust, so it is important for both parties to seek guidance for restoring trust to their relationship over time. But with God all things are possible—including saved marriages.

Marriage counselor Dr. Forrest Mobley told me (Quin) that he considers busyness one of the main problems facing marriages today. "We are too busy with things that take time from each other—binge-watching TV or spending hours on social media, rather than spending face-to-face time with our own spouse," he said.

He counsels couples that want to strengthen their marriages to pray together daily, to read the Bible together and discuss it, and to talk about the day ahead. "Most of all, we need to become dependent on a covenantal relationship with Jesus," he concluded.

Confronting Abuse

Some years ago, Carmen shared with us her experience of enduring what she called a hellish marriage. Steve married her because she was pregnant with his child, but he would humiliate her without any regard for her feelings. After ten years of frustration, she got involved in an affair with a man she met at church.

"Of course I realized later how badly deceived I was," she said. "When I learned my lover's best friend was going to expose the affair, I decided to confess to Steve. When he asked why I'd done it, I told him it was because he never expressed love to me and I was starving for someone to value me, to give me a sense of self-worth."

After repenting for her sin and making a new commitment to the Lord, Carmen asked God whether she could leave her unhappy marriage. God challenged her: *Are you willing to be made willing to love your husband unconditionally? And to treat him with as much love and kindness as you would Me, the Lord Jesus?*

Her answer was yes, she was willing to be loving and kind, even if she didn't receive love and kindness in return. But she felt the Lord would not require her to be treated like a doormat. So when Steve berated her, she simply replied firmly but kindly, "Don't talk to me like that, Steve—your attack is unwarranted." After several such responses, her husband began to change. One time he came into the kitchen and said, "I'm sorry for what I said. Will you forgive me?" And of course she did.

When Carmen stopped lashing out at Steve's angry words, Steve saw that he could not get into a fight and would back down. By establishing boundaries, Carmen earned his respect. She would embrace him and say, "This behavior really is beneath you—I know you're a loving, caring man." The Lord helped Carmen respond to Steve's hurtful words with a right spirit, and over time, he became kinder in his treatment of her. Today they have a solid marriage and are enjoying their grandchildren together.

An abusive husband is obsessed with trying to control his wife's behavior by using emotional manipulation—accusations, blame shifting, anger, threats, tears or even silence—because he wants to feel as if he is in charge. Putting the focus on her behavior rather than on his own faults or weaknesses, he may falsely accuse her of the very sins in which he himself is involved. He tries to isolate her from family and friends, intimidating her so that she feels powerless to stop the mistreatment or find help.

When verbal and emotional abuse continues unchallenged, it often escalates to increasingly serious attacks of physical abuse. These episodes frequently are followed by apologies and promises that it will never happen again. But more often than not, it does happen again. Instead of clinging to the hope that this time he means it, a woman in such a relationship must refuse to be manipulated.

Yes, Scripture mandates that we forgive those who offend or betray us, but we believe that a woman who is being verbally, emotionally or physically abused should take action to protect herself while fighting this spiritual battle. One minister advises the following:

1. **Pray for the abuser.** People who continually hurt others are in bondage to their own sin. And while that in no way excuses them, it gives you insight into how to pray for them. God intended these relationships for good, but they are undermined by alcohol, anger and other counterfeits Satan uses to destroy fellowship and family. Pray for the abuser to become the person God intended.

2. **Take a firm stand.** You may need group support and a mediator present for an intervention. God's light can penetrate the deepest darkness with hope, restoration and reconciliation, and when that happens, it is a quicker path to healing. Nevertheless, you need to take a firm stand—and if need be, get others to help you.

3. **Ask God, "Should I stay or go?"** It would be naïve to suggest that an intervention, sprinkled with prayer, will suddenly change everything. Some people respond to confrontation; some are melted by God's love. But many remain toxic and abusive, even when confronted in love, forgiven and drenched in grace. You may need to end the relationship, as difficult as that may be. Remember, it is not your job to change the person, and it is not a failure on your part if they do not change.[6]

Surviving Divorce

Unfortunately, some marriages do fail, no matter how much prayer or forgiveness is extended. God does not force obedience; a spouse might choose the wrong path, leaving the Christian wife or husband no recourse but to dissolve the marriage.

This is what happened to Lynne. Before their wedding, her fiancé, Dane, assured her that he was a believer; only afterward did she realize his deception. For eleven years, Lynne prayed for Dane's salvation. At times he went to church with her, but nothing in his life reflected a Christlike change.

After Dane retired from the military, they moved to the Middle East, where he worked for private industry and drew a huge salary. Consumed with greed, he stashed his money in Swiss bank accounts and invested in stocks and properties. These assets were placed in the names of various members of his family, but Lynne found out much later that nothing was in her name.

While Dane's life was spinning out of control because of his alcoholism, Lynne drew closer and closer to the Lord. One time, after Dane had been on a six-day drunken binge, Lynne heard what sounded like demons screaming through her husband, saying, "Go in and kill her! Go in and kill her! Go in and kill her!" She ran for her life.

Later she went back home, but Dane, who had been trained in psychological warfare, began using those tactics on Lynne. He would tell lies about her, calling her a spiritualist, and he almost succeeded in turning her parents and sons against her.

"I know God hates divorce, and I kept telling Dane I was committed to keeping our marriage together," she said, "but one day he filed divorce papers. Then I recognized that his heart was hardened, not only against me, but also against God. And he denied he had an alcohol problem."

Lynne learned God will not overwhelm the will of a person who refuses to yield his heart to the Lord. Neither could she argue her husband into the Kingdom. The divorce was granted, with Lynne receiving only three years of alimony.

"The Lord has provided a meaningful life and ministry for me over the years since the divorce," she said. "I had stood on the Word and declared Dane's salvation for so long, it became like an idol to me. I had to totally relinquish him to the Lord, with the prayer that someday, maybe when he hits bottom, he will see his need for Jesus. In the meantime, I'm going on with God and trusting Him to meet my needs."

Even for a newly divorced Christian like Lynne, God can provide peace and strength as she continues to look to Him. But it is also wise for a person in her circumstances to seek counseling to help her or him avoid the mistakes divorced people commonly make. According to Dr. Archibald Hart, these mistakes include:

- Condemning themselves, which intensifies their unhappiness
- Not dealing with guilt feelings in a constructive way
- Changing things too quickly, making adjustment even more difficult for all concerned
- Making promises they cannot keep
- Forcing the children involved to make painful choices
- Acting without a sense of self-awareness[7]

Avoiding Temptation

It is not always the men who get caught in the adultery trap, of course. We hear reports of women who get involved with a co-worker or the boss at work, a trainer at the health spa, their pastor, their best friend's husband or even someone they meet in an internet chat room. Of course, most of these women do not plan to have an affair. But they do not take precautions against it, either, and they fall into the trap.

"Beware of letting a male become your confidant," warns one woman who had a five-year affair with her married boss. She was devastated when he announced he was taking a job in another city and that their relationship was finished. She turned to the Bible for comfort, recommitted her life to Christ and set about saving her marriage.

In her book *Feelings Women Rarely Share*, Judy Reamer offers this analysis of sexual temptation for a woman:

> When a woman is not being emotionally satisfied in her marriage, she often begins to fantasize what another lifestyle may be like. Even though she may have a satisfying physical relationship with her husband, she still may feel deprived in the area of intimacy. She may be married to the strong, silent type who does not communicate or listen to what she is trying to say. Or she may be married to a selfish or demanding man who is a taker rather than a giver. . . . When unmet needs are combined with daydreams and fantasies, women become extremely vulnerable for an affair. . . .
>
> Whether your source of sexual temptation is an old boyfriend, a man on the job, or only someone you have had a dream about, the solution is still the same . . . stop the thoughts. Nip them in the bud . . . do not let your imagination run away with you. . . . Affairs start in the head before they get to the bed.[8]

Meditation on the Word of God—a weapon sharper than any two-edged sword—helps us get out of and stay out of immoral relationships.

With the help of the Holy Spirit, a difficult marriage actually can become a laboratory in which God's love has the power to bring restoration. When both partners are willing to cooperate with God, undergo changes and grow stronger in their walk with the Lord, wholeness can take place. Reconciliation can begin even when only one partner takes the initiative.

Marriage problems have no easy answers. But it is possible to build God-honoring relationships on a foundation of sacrificial love and a willingness to receive God's help and healing.

Speaking of healing, in the next chapter, we will look at ways to pray and battle during a health crisis.

Prayer for a Believing Husband

Lord, thank You for the marriage partner You have blessed me with. Help me to revere, honor and trust him and to speak with wisdom, but always with the law of kindness on my tongue. May my husband love me as Christ loves the Church, and together may we serve You faithfully. Give us a deeper understanding of Your Word as we seek to live by its standards and seek Your direction for our family. I pray that my husband will increase in wisdom and favor with You and his working associates and that he will reach his full potential as a man of God. Protect him from the fiery darts of the evil one. Help him to be the father and grandfather You intend for him to be, a godly influence and a blessing to all who know him [see Proverbs 31:23–26; Ephesians 1:17]. *Amen.*

Prayer for an Unbelieving Husband

Lord, it grieves me that my husband is not serving You, but I know You love him and desire to bring him to salvation. May he see Jesus reflected in my life. Help me to see him with Your eyes and love him with Your love. Lord, I pray You will send a godly man to share the gospel with him in a way he can understand and receive. In the name of

Jesus, I bind all evil spirits that are keeping my husband from knowing his heavenly Father. Grant him repentance leading to the knowledge of the truth, that he may come to his senses and escape from the snare of the devil, having been held captive by him to do his will. Lord, open his eyes so that he can turn from darkness to light and from the dominion of Satan to Your Kingdom, receiving forgiveness of sins. Thank You, Lord, for working in his life until this prayer is answered [see Acts 26:18; Romans 5:5; 2 Timothy 2:25–26 NASB]. *In Jesus' name, Amen.*

11

Healing and Spiritual Warfare

Jesus called his twelve disciples to him and gave them authority
to drive out impure spirits and to heal every disease and sickness.

Matthew 10:1

Paula and Jim rejoiced when their granddaughter, Tiffany, was
born. But three days later she had a seizure, and doctors told
the family, "The right front side of her brain is destroyed." So
these grandparents went into warfare mode to battle against
the enemy's plan to kill or cripple Tiffany.

They began a barrage of prayer using the Word of God.
"Satan, you have no legal right to attack this baby—she is bone
of my bone and flesh of my flesh," Jim would declare.

The Holy Spirit prompted him to pray about the blood supply
to the baby's brain. "God, put a new blood supply to the part
of Tiffany's brain that is damaged," he prayed. "Thank You

for hearing me. Thank You for doing it. New blood supply to her brain, Lord, new blood supply. Thank You, Lord."

After some time, when they felt God's peace and a sense of release, they stopped their warring. Soon a nurse came to tell Jim and Paula that the baby had stopped having seizures. When Jim asked what time the seizures had stopped, he learned it was the exact moment he had sensed it was time to stop battling.

Four days later, Tiffany went home from the hospital and never had another symptom. When her parents took her for her six-month checkup, the doctors said new blood had gone to the part of her brain that had been damaged, just as Jim had prayed. Tiffany never had another seizure and tested above normal in her development.

Paula and Jim covered Tiffany in prayer during her growing-up and college years, and they continue to do so now that she is married and a mom herself.

There Is No Formula

Just as there is no formula for spiritual warfare, Scripture does not provide a one-two-three formula for healing. Sometimes healing comes by the casting out of demons, sometimes by the faith of the person who is ill, sometimes by the laying on of hands, sometimes by a prayer of agreement—but always by Jesus' sovereign, supernatural touch.

Three such outstanding healings that Jesus performed in Galilee are recorded in the fifth chapter of Mark. The first involved a man tormented by evil spirits (see verses 1–20). He lived among the tombs and had such supernatural strength that no chains could hold him. Then he encountered Jesus and fell at His feet. Jesus commanded the evil spirits to come out of the man and go into a herd of pigs. Immediately the man was restored to his right mind.

Next is the account of a woman who had been bleeding for twelve years but had not been able to be helped by doctors (see verses 24–34). Pressing through the crowds around Jesus, she reached out and touched His cloak. Immediately her bleeding stopped. Jesus told her, "Daughter, your faith has healed you. Go in peace and be freed from your suffering" (verse 34).

The third healing concerned Jairus's young daughter (see verses 21–24, 35–43). While on the way to Jairus's house to heal the girl, Jesus heard that the child was dead. But Jesus said, "Do not be afraid; only believe" (verse 36 NKJV). With the girl's mother and father and His own disciples, Jesus entered the room where the child was lying. Taking her by the hand, He commanded, "Little girl, I say to you, get up!" (verse 41). The twelve-year-old stood up, walked around and then ate a meal. She was not just healed, but brought back to life.

God's power to heal certainly has not diminished today. Sometimes He uses doctors and modern medical technology, as well as prayer and spiritual warfare, to bring about healing. I (Ruthanne) once interviewed a surgeon who used to be outraged when he saw ministers praying for the sick.

"I felt they were infringing on my territory," he said. "I figured they should stick to preaching and let me and my professional colleagues in medicine take care of the sick.

"But then I became aware of the work of the Holy Spirit. When a Kathryn Kuhlman meeting came to our city, they invited me to sit on the platform. I watched as a woman who was bent over, crippled by disease and in constant pain was healed before my eyes. I could hear her bones snap as she stood up straight and began to walk freely, praising God. After that I began praying for my patients and realized I needed God's partnership in trying to help them."

Another respected Christian doctor gives this perspective on divine healing:

With God there is no universal, cookie-cutter, one-size-fits-all approach to healing. Just as no two people on earth have identical fingerprints, no two individuals will have exactly the same pathway to healing! . . .

God may use traditional medicine, a mineral, a plant, an herb. He may use something as commonplace as the vitamins and chemicals in certain foods, or something as dramatic as a surgical procedure. . . . For me, the key is praying and being open to the revelation and leading of the Holy Spirit.[1]

Scripture does not provide a fixed formula for healing. Because this is true, in every situation we face where spiritual warfare is called for, we need God's direction for wisdom and discernment. And that includes when we battle for any kind of healing. Here are brief accounts of three friends who shared the strategies God gave them as they stood in faith for their healing:

- Before seeing a doctor about her persistent headaches and dizziness, Judy and her husband went away to fast and pray for three days to seek God's wisdom and direction. Judy agreed to have surgery to remove a large brain tumor but knew she had to put her trust in God for complete recovery. She believes those days of fasting and seeking God prepared her for the battle. After eight weeks of recuperation, she left on a missions trip and never returned to her secular job. She has been involved in ministry ever since.

- Esther had had surgery four times to remove a growth under her arm that kept growing back. The doctor said that if it came back again, it probably would become cancerous. Esther had been praying for healing, but when the growth returned a fifth time, she determined to trust God instead of returning to the doctor. Then she dreamed about a group of people standing around a coffin and herself inside of it. In the dream, she began rebuking and binding Satan, declaring he could not take her life. Next, she saw an evil figure on the flatcar of a train being quickly taken away. She woke up, certain she was healed—and when she felt for the tumor under her arm, it was gone.

- Peggy was almost killed when a hit-and-run dune-buggy driver hit her as she opened her car door to get inside the vehicle. The impact sent her flying through the air until she hit her car's windshield and then fell onto the street. She heard a bystander praying for her, and in the ambulance she and her husband prayed the Lord's Prayer. Doctors stitched up the severed arteries in her leg but said she would need surgery the next day because she had a skull fracture and internal bleeding. The next morning, when her pastor came to pray and give her Holy Communion, she felt the power of the Holy Spirit as she took the sacrament. She knew she was healed. The doctor ordered new tests and soon returned to tell her the bleeding had stopped and surgery was not necessary. Peggy had a full recovery.

In these three examples, each woman came through her crisis by way of a different prayer strategy. These strategies required them to stay focused on their faith that God would give the victory as they resisted the enemy's attacks on their minds. In our next story, Arlene shares the useful principles she learned for winning the battle of the mind.

The Mind Is a Battlefield

God's best is for us to walk in divine health. However, many complex factors—some of them our fault, some of them the work of the enemy—frustrate God's highest plan for our lives. But one thing is clear in Scripture: The devil's intent always is "to steal and kill and destroy" (John 10:10).

Scripture indicates that the mind is a battlefield, so it is important for an effective spiritual warrior to learn how to stand against the enemy and "take captive every thought to make it obedient to Christ" (2 Corinthians 10:5).

When she learned she was in the final, hopeless stages of multiple sclerosis, Arlene had a dream one night in which she saw an open grave.[2] She knew the grave was hers, and fear squeezed her into the darkness. Then she heard a voice say, "Don't look down. Look up!" She awoke mystified and asked the Lord what the dream meant.

In her spirit, she heard His reply: *Arlene, don't focus on the circumstances. Don't look at your problem. Look at Me. Look at My resources. Look at My love. Don't look down. Look up!*

Arlene learned the futility of calling détente with Satan.

"We can't say to him, 'You leave me alone and I'll leave you alone,'" she said. "When we don't see a way out, our hearts falter and we find ourselves right where the devil wants us. He sucks us into the mire of helplessness and a no-win situation."

After the Lord gave her that dream, Arlene began to trust God to do the impossible as she resisted the oppression of the enemy against her mind and as she declared the truth of God's Word. Just as Nehemiah saw victory by refusing to go to the plain of Ono to talk with the enemy who was taunting him (see Nehemiah 6:2–3), Arlene experienced victory as she followed the Lord's instructions to her. She filled her thoughts with Scripture and resisted Satan's tormenting thoughts. Some time later, when she attended a healing service, she instantly was made whole.

Here are the principles God taught Arlene that night about His divine perspective:

In the Spirit	In the Natural
Seated in heavenly places	In the plain of "Oh no!"
Alert and active	Drowsy and inactive
Beholding Him	Focusing on the problem

In the Spirit	In the Natural
Moving in divine revelation	Listening to Satan's mockery
Receiving the Kingdom	Calling détente
Confident of victory	Defeated

"No matter how defeated you may have felt in the past, no matter how your mind has been assailed by the enemy, change your mind to agree with God's best," Arlene said. "Recognize that 'we have the mind of Christ' [1 Corinthians 2:16], and look up to see His triumph."

Arlene learned the power of focusing on the Word of God instead of the adversity in her life, as Smith Wigglesworth exemplified in his remarkable ministry of healing in the last century. He wrote:

> Believers are strong only as the Word of God abides in them. The Word of God is spirit and life to those who receive it in simple faith. . . . Know your Book, live it, believe it, and obey it. Hide God's Word in your heart. It will save your soul, quicken your body, and illumine your mind. . . . Inactivity of faith is a robber which steals blessing. Increase comes by action, by using what we have and what we know.[3]

The Fight for a Family

We firmly believe there is no situation that is beyond God's intervention. That includes infertility. Our friend James Goll and his late wife, Michal Ann, when they were a young barren couple, wanted desperately to become parents.

Into their fourth year of marriage, James had a dream in which the Holy Spirit told him he would have a son and that his son's name would be Justin. Months passed with no sign of pregnancy, but they continued trusting, not just in the dream but in the God of the dream.

The next year, Michal Ann underwent extensive tests to determine the cause of her barrenness. Their doctor, a top infertility specialist in the Midwest, concluded there were so many complications, it was not possible for her to have children.

James and Michal Ann decided to turn the diagnosis into this persistent prayer: *God, You gave us Your holy Word. You gave us a dream. We have believing people of prayer agreeing with us. We are totally dependent on You to bring it to pass. Fulfill the dream You gave us. Give us a miracle in the great name of Jesus.*

"We depleted every option we could think of in our search for an answer," Michal Ann said. "Most of all, we prayed, then rebuked our barrenness and declared God's Word over our bodies. Although we did everything we knew to do physically, medically and spiritually, still, after six years we ended up with no fruit. Let me tell you, it was incredibly painful."

Sometime later, when a healing evangelist visited their church, James and Michal Ann went for prayer. Afterward, the evangelist said to her, "Oh, I see you as a joyful mother of three children."

James recalls, "The presence of the Lord Jesus was so strong and tangibly powerful that we were unable to stand. Or perhaps we dropped to the floor out of shock. We had been trying to believe God for one child. Now the evangelist said he saw three."

Soon after the first of the year, Michal Ann thought she had the flu. But following an examination, her doctor delivered the good news, telling her, "You're going to have a baby."

They were elated, shocked, thrilled. On October 4, 1983, Justin Wayne Goll was born, followed by GraceAnn, Tyler and finally Rachel, who was a real surprise!

The Lord had spoken to Michal Ann's heart that she must fight for her children. James says the children came as a result of prayer, fighting the enemy and supernatural acts of God's power. He believes God wants to heal other barren women just as He healed Michal Ann.[4]

The War for Life

Fran was a woman of faith who learned a new depth of spiritual warfare when her husband needed emergency heart surgery. Mike had been in a wheelchair for 35 years as a result of polio. He was now a 67-year-old triplegic with heart complications. Though doctors said Mike's chances of survival were minimal, they air-evacuated him to a large medical center for surgery.

A prayer partner called to give Fran this verse to encourage Mike: "When I passed by you and saw you squirming in your blood, I said to you while you were in your blood, 'Live!'" (Ezekiel 16:6 NASB).

"Mike, do you want to live?" Fran asked her husband the night before surgery. "I don't want you to be praying to die while I'm praying for you to live. I want to honor what you want, because things could get rough in this battle."

"I want to live, Fran," Mike assured her. "I feel God has some things left for me to do. I love life, so of course I want to live."

Holding his hand, Fran prayed aloud, "Lord, we now agree and declare *Mike chooses life*. If we hit any tight places in the days ahead, we are in agreement with Your word to Mike that he does choose life!"

The surgery went smoothly, and when doctors felt all was under control, they allowed Mike to make the six-hour trip back to his home. But the first night home, he began to hemorrhage and was rushed to the local hospital. They stabilized Mike's condition with transfusions, but over the next forty days, he fought for his life. Doctors pumped fifteen units of blood into him.

One night after Mike was moved to a private room, he began hemorrhaging again. Fran called for help, and a medical team hurried to get IVs going in his arms, legs and chest. He had no detectable blood pressure, and his vascular system was collapsing. Fran, a nurse, knew he was dying.

While the medical team was working, she knelt down and looked Mike in the eye. Though he could not respond, she knew he could hear her.

"Mike, choose life!" she shouted. "Choose life, Mike! Choose life . . . choose life . . . choose life. You will not die but live. Choose life!"

She watched Mike's eyes until she was sure he understood. Even though he could not breathe on his own, she knew that both fight and light had come back into him.

During Mike's long hospital stay, prayer warriors gathered outside his room day and night to join Fran in fighting for his life. They would pray, recite Bible verses aloud and declare to the devil that he was not going to snuff out Mike's life prematurely. He would live.

And live, he did! For the next eighteen years, Mike had an active life in his wheelchair, and God used him and Fran to teach and mentor many people through Bible studies in their home.

The Time for Release

While the examples of healing we have shared are primarily victories, healing does not always come. Most of us have family members or friends we prayed would be healed, but they did not recover. We do not have answers as to why this happens, but it is only realistic to acknowledge that the time will come when we all will die.

We know of numerous cases where the loved one being prayed for asked the family to release him or her, as they were ready to go home to heaven. I (Ruthanne) have often shared with friends facing this painful situation that they ask God to give their loved one an abundant entrance into His presence (see 2 Peter 1:11 NKJV).

On one occasion, my church scheduled a special night when prayer for healing would be offered, and I was serving on the prayer team. A woman in a wheelchair who was battling lung cancer asked for prayer. I anointed her with oil and prayed healing Scriptures over her, and I encouraged her husband to read those verses to her in the days ahead. A short time later, I learned the woman had passed away. However, her husband shared with one of our pastors that his wife had been in torment before she received prayer that night. But that in the final days of her life, she was calm, was not suffering and had a peaceful passing.

As we trust God to allow us to live out our days on the earth to do His will, often a spiritual battle will be required. But from our study of the Bible, we continue to believe it is our business to pray and God's business to heal, in His way and in His timing. He still gives His followers authority to drive out evil spirits and heal sickness in His mighty name. Let's not stop!

Intercessors often ask us, "How can I recognize when I am under attack?" In the next chapter, we will explore this topic.

Prayer

Father, I give You thanks for the promise of Scripture declaring that Jesus bore our sins on the cross and that by His stripes we are healed [see 1 Peter 2:24]. I choose to believe Your Word, and I put my trust in You for healing for [name]. Lord, if there is pride, unforgiveness, disobedience or unbelief obstructing the flow of Your healing power, please reveal it and give grace for repentance and correction. Strengthen my faith as I fill my mind with Scripture and wait upon You for direction and strategy. Father, I choose to keep my focus upon You and to find joy in each day You give. Thank You. In Jesus' name, Amen.

12

Are You under Attack?

Beloved, do not think it strange concerning the fiery trial which is to try you, as though some strange thing happened to you; but rejoice to the extent that you partake of Christ's sufferings.

1 Peter 4:12–13 NKJV

By now you have discovered that just because you are a Christian, you are not immune to the attacks of the evil one. But you have a direct line to the One who can free you and heal you and give you a strategy to overcome it.

How do you know if you are under attack? How can you discern whether evil forces are at work in your life or if it is God at work? One teacher suggests that you ask yourself, *Is what I am experiencing a temptation, a test or an attack?*

- If it is a *temptation*, I want to resist! I could choose to say as Joseph did when tempted by Potiphar's wife, "How then could I do such a wicked thing and sin against God?" (Genesis 39:9).
- If it is a *test* sent by the Lord to teach me something, I want to learn.

- But if it is an *attack from Satan*, I want to fight to see his plan defeated.[1]

Does God test us and teach us? Yes. We read of His dealings with Israel: "These are the nations the Lord left to test all those Israelites who had not experienced any of the wars in Canaan (he did this only to teach warfare to the descendants of the Israelites who had not had previous battle experience)" (Judges 3:1–2). God wanted the younger Israelites to learn war through hands-on experience.

We need to ask God what it is He wants us to learn in the situations we are facing and ask Him for strategy to overcome any difficulty. Then we need to trust Him to show us what He wants us to learn or do.

"What Is This, Lord?"

JoAnne, an intercessor for a major Christian ministry, awoke one morning feeling as if she had been kicked in the head by a horse. In moments, she was partially paralyzed. Rousing her sleeping husband, a military doctor, she told him, "You'd better get me to the hospital; I can't move!"

While waiting for the ambulance, JoAnne began praying, *Lord, are You about to take me home? If You are, I'm ready. But if this is an attack from Satan, I need to know so I can fight. Which is it?*

An attack! She felt she had heard God's word.

Lord, I know what to do with an attack—fight. And I'll fight for all I'm worth because that means You have something greater in mind for me, she prayed. *Now, please strengthen me to fight.*

Stand. I'm in this with you, the Lord seemed to assure her.

During the next few days in the hospital, whenever she would feel another swift "kick in the head," JoAnne would declare, "Satan, you've come far enough. You can't kill me. I'm hidden in Jesus. By His stripes I am healed. Now back off!" Then she would sing and worship God for a long time.

Although doctors ran numerous tests and even sent her to an out-of-state hospital, they never diagnosed JoAnne's illness. The only abnormality the doctors found was a smaller-than-normal artery in her head, possibly a condition she had had since birth. One doctor told her plainly, "I do not know what is wrong." Finally the paralysis and excruciating headaches left her, and she went back to her usual routine.

But whenever JoAnne feels another swift blow to her head, she knows it is an attack from Satan. She says, "Devil and every demon spirit coming against my body to give me this infirmity, I tell you to stop your maneuvers in the name of my Savior, Jesus Christ. You are a defeated foe, and I am redeemed by the blood of Jesus." She continues to walk in victory today, and she mentors other women in warfare and intercession.

"Am I Doing Something Wrong?"

Once I (Ruthanne) was teaching on spiritual warfare for a women's group in East Texas. Afterward a woman shared that in her two-year walk with the Lord, she had led several family members to accept the Lord—she was one of the first in the clan to become a Christian. But now she was troubled about many serious problems she and her family were facing.

"Am I doing something wrong?" she asked.

"No, it's not that you're doing anything wrong," I assured her. "Your praying and witnessing have made you a prime target for the enemy because you're invading his territory. Actually, you should be encouraged to know you are a threat to the devil's kingdom. Take up your weapons and fight!"

The following chart contrasts the characteristics of these two types of trial:

Enemy Attack	God's Correction
Accusation, condemnation of you	Conviction concerning an attitude or deed
Depression	Call to repentance
Hopelessness	Assurance of forgiveness
Destruction of self-esteem	Restoration of a sense of your value as God's child

I helped the woman with guidelines and Scriptures to go along with the lesson I had just taught, and I prayed with her and encouraged her to find a prayer partner to stand with her in warfare concerning her family problems.

Her question—"Am I doing something wrong?"—is a question all of us ask at one time or another. How do we tell whether we have gotten off track somewhere or are under enemy attack? Is the enemy opposing us, or is God trying to tell us something?

I asked some seasoned, godly women for wisdom in this area.

"When the enemy attacks, there is great condemnation and seemingly no way out," a pastor's wife told me. "I distinguish by recognizing the difference between condemnation and conviction. Condemnation brings hopelessness. When the Holy Spirit convicts, there is a way out. I can confess my sin—of gossip, lying or whatever—and receive forgiveness and cleansing."

"The enemy will try to defeat us in some area or even remove us from the spiritual race entirely," another friend said. "God's correction, on the other hand, exposes a heart condition or weakness in some area. His correction gets us a better place in the race and keeps us in focus for the next battle."

"I have contested and rebelled against God's roadblocks," a young graduate student told me. "But I knew that I was acting in defiance of God rather than against the crippling influence of evil. Attacks by evil forces generally have been accompanied by a spiritual prompting for prayer against the opposition."

"How Does the Enemy Gain Access?"

We asked more than a hundred intercessors, "What makes a believer vulnerable to the enemy's attack?" They mentioned these major ways we can give the enemy access to our hearts, minds and bodies:

- Sin (immoral behavior, disobedience, anger, pride, rebellion, unforgiveness, criticism, selfishness and so on)
- Ignorance of Satan's devices and characteristics
- Compromise with the enemy
- Limited knowledge of God's Word and His purposes
- Not spending time with the Lord (lack of discipline and vigilance, becoming careless or passive)
- Lack of persistence or focus in discerning between the voices we hear
- Failure to use spiritual weapons (due to the above reasons)
- Taking our eyes off Jesus and focusing instead on our problems
- Immaturity (blind spots or areas of our lives not yielded to the lordship of Jesus)
- Fatigue (physical, emotional or spiritual)
- Preoccupation with self and physical comfort
- Inadequate prayer coverage by others
- Disunity or contention with fellow Christians and in the home

Sometimes, however, there seems to be no chink in your armor, no disobedience to God, no willful sinning, when—*pow*—here comes an arrow aimed at putting you out of existence.

Rowena felt like that when a drunk driver hit her car, causing serious injuries. God showed her the accident was definitely an arrow from the bow of the enemy. Since the Bible says "no weapon forged against you will prevail" (Isaiah 54:17), Rowena claimed that verse as she began her long convalescence. She also meditated on Psalm 23:4: "Though I walk through the valley of the shadow of death, I will fear no evil" (NKJV). When doctors said she might never walk again, she clung to that Scripture and used it in warfare. And she did walk again.

Five years later, she had another car wreck. She was able to get out of the car and run to safety just before her car rolled over an embankment and was totaled.

"This time, a righteous indignation arose in me," Rowena said. "I found that once again I had to put a guard on my mind by quoting Scriptures to resist fear that my life might be totally destroyed. Only a renewed mind can rise up in times of attack and defeat the purposes of the enemy."

Over the years, we have prayed with women who seem to have a pattern of repeated attacks of a certain kind within their families—divorce, addictions, car accidents, falls or other mishaps, miscarriages or abortions, occult activity and more. In many cases, this is because of generational bondages that need to be addressed. If you become aware of repeated problems in these areas, ask the Lord for direction and strategy to deal with them. (See chapter 8 for more details regarding this issue.)

Satan's Counterfeits

As our society becomes more and more materialistic, cynical about absolute authority and charitable toward false religions, people are fooled into believing they can "be like God." This concept is the basic belief of New Age philosophy.

Discernment is our safeguard against deception. A deceived mind can lead us astray (see Isaiah 44:20 AMP), and the apostle Paul wrote that "Satan himself masquerades as an angel of light" (2 Corinthians 11:14). Many Scriptures warn us how easily we can be deceived, not only by false religions, but also by our selfish desires that are not in alignment with God's purposes (see James 1:14–15).

One time at a retreat, I (Quin) spoke on prayer and mentioned the power of agreement. Afterward, a beautiful blonde came up to ask for prayer.

"Pray in agreement with me for my husband," she said.

"What is his name?" I asked.

"Oh, I'm not married," she answered. "I moved here a few months ago because I believe God told me I'd find my husband here. I received a prophecy from someone I don't know who said my ministry will not go far until I'm married. I want my ministry to flourish, and I want to be married."

"Sorry to disappoint you, but I cannot pray in agreement with you for this," I told her. "I will pray for God's plan and purpose to be accomplished in your life. But I have not had opportunity to pray about your situation and ask God for His leading as to whether I should pray for you to find your husband in this town."

The woman looked shocked and hurt because I would not pray for her husband to come forth from wherever he was. But I did stop right then and pray for God to fulfill His plan for her life. We are always safe to pray for God's destiny for someone and to ask the Holy Spirit to reveal His will for that person. After all, Jesus taught us to pray, "Thy kingdom come, thy will be done on earth."[2]

We need to stay self-controlled and alert to avoid the enemy's tactics to pull us off guard and into his camp. The apostle Peter warns us to resist the devil and stand firm in faith (see 1 Peter 5:8–9).

"Whose Voice Is That?"

Women have often shared with us experiences of hearing a voice and wondering whether it was from God or not. Actually, there are three possibilities:

1. It could be God speaking through the Holy Spirit. If so, whatever is spoken will be consistent with God's character and His Word.
2. It could be a demonic voice representing Satan.
3. It could be your own inner voice "speaking" a thought based on your logical reasoning, your will and human desire, or your self-centered emotions.

If you have difficulty discerning which it might be, we suggest this warfare prayer:

Lord, I desire to hear Your voice and be led by You. If this is Your Holy Spirit speaking, please cause this impression I have to become clearer and more urgent. If You want me to take any action, cause the urge to do this thing to increase. If this impression I have is not of You, please cause it to fade. By the authority of the blood of Jesus that covers me, I command any evil spirits present to be silent, in Jesus' name, and to flee. I silence the voice of my own reasoning, desires and feelings. I refuse to hear any alien voice; I will listen only to the voice of my Shepherd. Thank You, Father, for speaking to me by whatever means You choose as I wait upon You. I promise to obey that which You speak. Amen.

When we say God's voice will be consistent with His character and His Word, we mean it. The difference between God's voice and the enemy's voice could not be more clear. Look at the difference through the lens of Ruby's story.

When the hospital nurse brought Ruby's newborn to her for the first time, she was repulsed by the sight of her four-and-a-half-pound preemie. He looked like an ugly, shriveled-up ninety-year-old man. In her mind she heard a voice say, *Throw him on the floor. You don't want him. Throw him on the floor.*

"I hugged him to my bosom and withdrew into a corner of the room as though to protect us both," Ruby recalled. "Since I had lost three babies through miscarriages, I had bargained with God for this baby, as Hannah did for her son, Samuel. Naming him Michael, for the warrior angel, I promised God he would be a mighty warrior for Him."

Ruby recognized that an enemy voice had told her to destroy her baby, and she refused to heed the order. "It was as real as any voice I've ever heard," she said. "I know God gives life; He doesn't destroy. So I had no trouble knowing this was not God but an attack from Satan himself, and I ordered him to leave."

Most of us know the enemy's voice is not always as clearly discernible as it was in Ruby's case, so it is important we spiritual warriors fill our minds with the Word of God and remain vigilant and aware of the enemy's devices.

One of the enemy's primary devices is fear, and he uses various ways to instill it in a person. One young newlywed shared how she became aware of the enemy's attempt to instill fear in her and how she learned to resist the attack.

"I was a new bride living in an unfamiliar city, and my husband traveled extensively," she said. "Satan used my loneliness as a means of instilling fear, subjecting me to a series of noises. For several months, whenever my husband was out of town, I'd be awakened in the night by the sound of my husband's voice and noises he would make while working in his office. I could hear drawers opening and closing and the computer clicking. Although I was wide awake, the sounds would continue for some time and in great detail. I was greatly troubled by it.

"After several months of such occurrences, I was led by the Lord to come directly against the devil's schemes in the name of Jesus Christ. As I did this repeatedly, the noises stopped and never recurred. I received a great deal of strength and confidence, and my fear was replaced by well-directed anger at the devil. I learned that persistent prayer renders Satan powerless, meaning his attack cannot continue."

These stories illustrate how important it is that we learn to discern between God's dealings *with* us and the devil's attacks *against* us. The next time you feel as if a ton of bricks has fallen on your head, you may want to ask, *God, is this a temptation, a test or an attack?* We desire to resist temptation, pass God's tests and fight any satanic attack.

Remember, every time you win a victory, you are strengthened and trained for the next battle, and God will open opportunities for you to help liberate other believers under attack. Yes, a woman's place is in the war!

In our closing chapter, we share some valuable lessons learned by other spiritual warriors that will encourage and instruct you as you find your place in this war.

Prayer

Father, just as Jesus prayed that You would protect His disciples from the evil one, I ask that You also protect me and my loved ones from the enemy. Teach us to clearly hear Your voice, see Your plan and follow Your direction. Teach us how to discern when we are under attack by the devil and how to use our weapons effectively. We love You, Lord, and our greatest desires are to serve You, to please You and to help set the captives free. Speak to our hearts, Lord, for Your servants are listening. In Jesus' name, Amen.

13

Lessons from the Field

No weapon that is formed against you shall prosper, and every tongue that shall rise against you in judgment you shall show to be in the wrong. This [peace, righteousness, security, triumph over opposition] is the heritage of the servants of the Lord [those in whom the ideal Servant of the Lord is reproduced]; this is the righteousness or the vindication which they obtain from Me [this is that which I impart to them as their justification], says the Lord.

Isaiah 54:17 AMPC

Women identify with other women dealing with problems unique to women. The following stories—lessons from the field—are actual experiences of godly women who have faced problems you may be facing now or may confront in the future.

In the Workplace

Both single and married women juggle work with family and other interests to contribute their share to the household.

Finding a job—much less the right job—is not always easy, either. But as Eunice learned, even when the job does not seem right at first, it may be exactly where God wants you.

With her children all enrolled in school, Eunice decided to return to her nursing career. She asked the Lord for a job where she could pray with patients who might be ready to receive Him. If she accepted the job she wanted on the cancer floor of the university hospital, her bosses would be the chief of the oncology unit and the head nurse. The two were having an affair, and both were known to be anti-Christian. Eunice wondered whether she should take the job, knowing it would involve tests and trials.

At her interview, Eunice asked the doctor point-blank, "Can I pray with patients?"

"Aw, go ahead," he snarled. "I need you here immediately, so you're hired."

As Eunice went on her nursing rounds, she prayed for any patient who wanted prayer. But working with a doctor and head nurse who mocked her God was a challenge. She often overheard them swearing and making fun of her for believing prayer could help anybody on a cancer ward. She did not argue with them; she just called on the Lord for strength to keep at it.

One day when Eunice felt she had been targeted for abuse, she heard the Lord whisper, *Don't let Satan remove you from where I've placed you and called you to stand.* So she determined to keep praying and not to give up.

A year later, the chief of the department and his head nurse were fired. Gradually, many other godless people were removed. Most were replaced by believers, and soon it was not unusual for several nurses to meet with Eunice in the supply room, their "prayer closet." They began talking openly to the patients about their Christian faith and have seen many come to know the Lord.

"It was anything but easy those first months," Eunice said. "The enemy wanted me to throw in the towel, but God wanted someone who could bring His life to the patients. I'm glad He helped me stick it out."

In Finances

With financial systems so unstable throughout the world, it seems that whenever my friends and I (Quin) meet for prayer, the cry is, "Lord, we need a financial breakthrough. We trust You to supply our needs. Come to our rescue!"

The downsizing and merging of companies have contributed to widespread job layoffs, which in turn has led to an increase in the number of houses in foreclosure and bankruptcies being declared. Obviously, there is a need for God's intervention.

When Linda and her husband moved to a smaller house, their larger one stood vacant almost nine months because the housing market had hit bottom. I knew they tithed their income and were a family dedicated to the Lord, so I joined her in praying the house would sell as we stood on God's promises to meet their needs.

One day while praying with her, the Lord dropped into my thoughts something entirely different from what I would have imagined.

"Let's pray for the family who needs that house, can afford it and will enjoy it immensely," I said to Linda. "We'll pray the new owners will have as much happiness there as you did while raising your family in that place."

So we prayed in agreement a blessing prayer over the future owners. I also suggested that Linda go back to her property and pray on-site.

Less than a week later, I got an excited call. The roomy two-story house had sold to a family with several children who needed to live near the military base. They loved the house because it was ideal for them. Greatly relieved, Linda and her husband called their friends to share their "Hallelujahs" for answered prayer.[1]

Unfortunately, many out-of-work families have not had their financial needs met that soon. Also, a lot of people have lost not only income but also most of their investment and retirement funds, since the bottom fell out of the stock market. Many retirees I know are struggling to stretch their income to meet their bills, especially medical expenses.

One prayer warrior whose husband lost his job told me, "I have learned I need to get a different strategy for every situation we face. Praying for finances and breaking the spirit of poverty are not the same. To break poverty, we made sure we tithed. We did everything we knew to fulfill the Word and stay in covenant with God so that Satan has no legal right to harass us. We also speak to the seed we've sown, asking God to restore what the enemy has stolen. What we lost shall be recovered."

The woman continued by pointing out the biblical example of David at Ziklag, when the enemy came in his absence, burned the city and took everyone captive. David was so discouraged, he wept and cried out to God. Then he strengthened himself in the Lord and asked God what to do. The Lord responded, "Pursue, for you shall surely overtake them and without fail recover all" (1 Samuel 30:8 NKJV). David and his men pursued and defeated the enemy, then recaptured everything that had been taken. He not only brought back the spoils, but he had enough to give to other cities.

"God wants to do that for us, too," the woman concluded. "I believe He will give us the needed warfare strategies to see victory."

In Compassion

A praying mom whose son is living in the gay world says her situation has caused her to look at homosexuals in a completely different light: as a challenge for prayer and warfare.

"My heart has been broken for my son, but I also weep for other young people—many from Christian homes—who are trapped in Satan's cruel deception," she wrote. "I can't see a gay person on the street or in a store without thinking, *I wonder if anyone is praying for him?*

"One time an acquaintance, who doesn't know about my son, commented about a homosexual working at the hair salon she goes to. 'I don't want him to even touch me,' she said with a shudder. I can't imagine Jesus ever making such a remark. Suppose the woman caught in adultery [see John 8:3] had been a male prostitute? Would Jesus have encouraged the crowd to stone the man?

"I used to be incensed about the gay activists I read about in the newspaper. Then the Lord told me to start praying for them, as well as their families. I learned that the former president of the gay-activist group in our city was the son of a Pentecostal pastor, and the leader who succeeded him was the son of an evangelical pastor. Both young men have since died of AIDS. As I prayed for them, God replaced my disdain with compassion for them and their families. How can we hope to win them if we treat them like lepers?"

In praying for our nation and the subcultures within it that so desperately need to see Jesus as He truly is, we must walk in compassion. John Dawson reminds us:

> As you stand in the gap for your city, allow the Holy Spirit to shine the bright truth into the inner rooms of your soul. Run from the religious deceit that would seduce you into believing that you are superior to any person. It is only by the blood of

the Lamb and the power of the Spirit that we stand free from the chains of guilt and the sentence of death.[2]

In Grief

The enemy often tries to use grief to paralyze a woman's emotions and nullify her Christian witness. If ever there was a woman who could have given in to her deep sorrow, it was Emily.

Emily was 27 when her test-pilot husband was killed. Crushed with grief, she blamed God for leaving her a widow with a four-year-old. Her mother told her, "Emily, Jesus is a good Shepherd, and you are one of His little lambs. He will take care of you. Just trust Him."

Emily's anger toward God lifted as she began to study the Word of God and discovered the Shepherd really did love her. She returned to college and began designing children's clothes. Six years later, she met a lawyer who proposed marriage.

"I knew I didn't love him like my first love, but by now I had grown in the Lord and could love him with God's love, so I married him," she said. "He was a kind, gentle man. But after we'd had sixteen years together, he died of a heart condition. Again I found myself a widow."

The Lord gave Emily this verse that helped her through her second bout of grief: "No one who puts a hand to the plow and looks back is fit for service in the kingdom of God" (Luke 9:62).

Emily has been a widow now for many years, and God has been a faithful husband to her as she presses closer and closer to Him. "I don't look back, because if I did, I would not accomplish what God has for me to do for Him today," she says. Her ministry is to head up the intercessory-prayer group at her large urban church.

Her advice for other widows is:

- Don't let bitterness, anger or grief rob you of a fulfilled life today. Release those feelings to God.
- Thank God for the spouse you had and for the good years you enjoyed together. Be grateful.
- Trust the Lord to meet your needs in the areas where you once depended on a husband.
- Read the Word of God, study it and get to know the Lord personally.
- Reach out to others, especially to other widows, and help bring healing into their lives.

In Discernment

Janet's six-year-old son, Kevin, came in from school one day with a defiant, sassy attitude. "What did you do in school today, son?" she asked, puzzled by his mood.

"Played with a crystal ball the teacher brought. We asked it all kinds of questions," he answered.

Lord, what shall I do about this? Janet, a new Christian, prayed silently. From deep within, she heard, *Break the witchcraft and curses that come with it.*

"Kevin, come sit on my lap for a minute," she said, still asking the Lord how to follow the direction she had just received. She gave Kevin a big hug as he climbed on her lap. Then she heard herself saying, "Father, in the name of Jesus, I break the power of witchcraft and curses, and I take back from the enemy the ground he has stolen from my son. We give that ground back to You, Lord. Thank You for Your protection and Your blessing upon Kevin."

After prayer, Kevin immediately changed back to her happy, sweet-natured kid.

"That was my introduction to dealing with invisible evil forces," Janet said. "In a nutshell, I quickly learned about spiritual warfare, and I'm still using it for both of my children."

When Kevin grew older, he began driving a huge cattle-transport truck-trailer across the country. One night Janet woke up four times, and each time she "saw" a truck going off the road. It was the eighteen-wheeler Kevin was driving.

"I began binding the spirits of death and calamity, and then I asked the Lord to send angels to keep my son's truck on the road," she remembers. "I did it four times that night."

At dawn Kevin called to say, "Mom, I'm back in town, but I'm too tired to drive home. Four times last night my truck almost went off the road. Were you praying?"

We need to be alert and sensitive to the Holy Spirit's nudging day and night, always available to do warfare and pray at a moment's notice.

In Vows

Sometimes women open themselves to oppression from the enemy when they take an oath as part of an initiation in a secret society. During Rae's first weeks at college, she was thrilled when a social club invited her to join. Against the advice of her pastor and parents, she accepted, paid her dues and made a pledge. But the more she attended the meetings and participated in the group's activities, the more frequent her headaches and depression became.

In prayer one day, she asked the Lord to show her the root cause. She heard, *You took vows inconsistent with your Christian faith.*

Rae repented, asked God's forgiveness and tried to get out of her commitment, only to be told she could not do it. She then called the national headquarters and demanded that her name be removed from the membership list, and she cancelled her vows.

"I was set free from guilt, depression and headaches—I knew I should never have joined that organization in the first place," she reported.

Others in similar circumstances may need to get rid of a ring or pin that symbolizes their vows or renounce in prayer their association with any secret organization that compromises their commitment to Christ.

In Cleansing

Any difficulty we or a family member faces in life gives us an opportunity to seek God's battle plan for resolving it.

Gloria was more than concerned because her daughter Tori, a dedicated Christian, was in conflict with her college roommate. The girls had been close friends in high school and had looked forward to rooming together, but now arguments and disagreements were too common.

One weekend when Gloria stayed overnight in the dorm with Tori while the roommate was away, she discovered two disturbing facts. First, the previous year a violent race riot had exploded in that very dorm room, leaving some students with bloody noses. Second, Tori's roommate had made a cross-stitched plaque and hung it over their door: "Dorm Bitter Dorm"—a takeoff on "Home Sweet Home."

"It seemed the room had been invaded with spirits of anger, hate, rage, resentment and murder—spirits that had been 'invited' through rioting the previous semester," Gloria said. "And the sign above the door didn't help matters; it was like putting out a welcome mat for a spirit of bitterness.

"Tori and I removed the sign; then using Jesus' name and authority, we commanded the unclean spirits to leave that room," she told us. "Tori asked the Lord to forgive her for her part in the strife with her roommate, and we asked God to fill the room with His peace. The results were almost immediate. It seemed the air had been cleansed, and a blanket of peace pervaded the room. The girls are no longer roommates, but they remain friends."

In Lust

While traveling on a ministry trip, Katherine was a guest in the home of a woman she had never met. As she put her suitcase in the guest-room closet, she was bombarded with lustful thoughts and feelings. She rebuked them, commanded that any evil spirits leave the room, then called her husband to pray for her. The thoughts left.

That evening she opened the closet to hang up her clothes, and once again lustful thoughts invaded her mind. When she pulled the string to turn on the light and let go of it, it flipped onto the top shelf of the closet. Reaching up to retrieve it, Katherine pulled down a couple of magazines on the top shelf that were blatantly pornographic. Now she understood why a spirit of lust had attacked her mind when she opened the closet.

After she showed her hostess what she had discovered, the woman told Katherine that she, too, had experienced lustful feelings whenever she cleaned that closet. The woman confronted her nineteen-year-old son, and he admitted this was his secret hiding place for his porn magazines. With the matter exposed, he agreed to counseling.

"Since then," Katherine said, "whenever I stay in a hotel or guest room, I make it a habit to command every unclean spirit that might be present to leave in the name and authority of Jesus Christ of Nazareth. All kinds of spirits dwell in hotel rooms where illicit sex, drug dealing, perversion and porn movies have been going on."

Once when I (Quin) checked in for a conference, the registration packet included the suggestion that each woman, once she got into her hotel room, declare aloud, "In Jesus' name, I renounce any claim to this room by Satan, based on activities of past occupants. I command all evil spirits to leave this place and never return." This is the recommended prayer that followed:

Heavenly Father, thank You for this room where we can fellowship and rest during our conference. I ask You to make this room a place of physical and spiritual safety for me and anyone else who enters it. I ask You, Lord God, to station holy, warring angels to set a guard around this room. Your Holy Spirit is welcome here. Send Him to bless us, even as we sleep in this place. Thank You. In Jesus' name, Amen.

In Missions

People who travel in ministry become aware of their need for prayer coverage as they work on the front lines of confrontation with the enemy. A young woman missionary, after her first term of service in Southeast Asia, wrote in her newsletter:

If folks at home don't pray for me, then I'd better stay at home! My reaction to my first term of service is that the mission field is like a fierce battlefield, in which there are no ceasefires. In an ordinary war, ground soldiers are not expected to fight unless sufficient air cover is provided; otherwise they might soon be wiped out.

Similarly, it seems to me to be equally irresponsible for a church to send someone out as its representative into the warfare of the mission field, if that church is unable or unwilling to maintain sufficient, continual praying forces to defeat the enemy attacks that strike missionaries continually.[3]

The need for prayer coverage applies in many situations: a loved one serving in the military or traveling and working in dangerous surroundings, a child at camp or college or living in a crime-ridden city, a Christian teacher trying to uphold godly standards in a public school classroom—the list goes on.

In Crisis

Most of us have seen horrific scenes blared across our television screens, showing the aftermath of evil deeds: innocents killed and wounded in bombings during a marathon; Christians gunned down while having a Bible study in a church; moviegoers killed in their seats; youth murdered in schools; unarmed military recruiters mowed down in cold blood. In some countries, Christians are imprisoned or killed just because they refuse to deny their faith in Christ, while others are randomly murdered by religious fanatics.

As we have mentioned throughout this book, we are called to be praying women, taking on the causes God puts on our hearts or rising up to do spiritual battle in unexpected circumstances. As intercessors, we stand before God on behalf of a person or situation, appealing for His intervention and mercy. But we also push back the forces of darkness—Satan and his demonic forces—and in the name and authority of Jesus declare, "No more. Back off. You have no right to this property." God even calls us to intercede for cities and nations.

The following is such an example.

Martha, a widow who serves in an international ministry, spent 25 years doing spiritual warfare and intercession in forty nations with praying teams. She had moved to England for five years, making her way through 39 counties with her teams.

"We exhorted believers at our meetings to rise up as a praying army of the Lord so that their land would not be taken over by false gods," she said. "They were encouraged to repent for any idolatry, innocent bloodshed, broken covenants, immorality or other sins they knew had taken place on the land."

Then on the morning of July 7, 2005, a series of coordinated suicide bombings occurred on three London underground trains, all within fifty seconds of each other. Martha and her associate, Sharon, were on a commuter train heading to a Christian meeting at the time and were soon among the crowds in the streets hurrying for safety.

Dragging their suitcases, they waited for a nearby pub to open and settled at a table. For the next seven hours, they prayed—in English and in their prayer languages.

"I asked the Lord to paralyze the terrorists—their hands, their arms, their plots and plans," Martha remembered. "We prayed for those still buried under the rubble of the explosions, for the police, firemen, ambulance workers and medics."

She and Sharon had no idea whether more bombings might be imminent, but they took authority over demonic forces, declaring they would not take any more lives. A television set in the pub gave sketchy updates, providing prayer points for them as the news unfolded and they learned a fourth bomb had exploded on a bus.

After those seven hours, they made their way by foot to their hotel, where the first floor had been turned into a triage center for the wounded to be brought for medical attention. When they told the officers who they were, they were allowed to pray for the wounded and the aid workers.[4]

Radical terrorists claimed responsibility for the attacks that day, when 56 people were killed (including the four bombers) and seven hundred were injured. Two other bombs were found that did not explode. Several days later, four more explosions took place at various locations, but while the fuses of all four of those bombs went off, none of the main explosive charges detonated. No casualities resulted from the second round of attacks, and the suspected bombers were later arrested. Also, more than a dozen unexploded bombs were found in a car at the Luton train station.

Of course, Martha and Sharon were not the only Christians on a prayer watch that infamous day—we know others were, too. But she says, "We are strategically positioned in the heavenlies with Christ by the Holy Spirit. Christ in us places us in a position to engage the enemies of God through spiritual warfare. We must settle in our own spirit the truth regarding our authority in Christ." (See Ephesians 2:6; 1 Peter 2:9.)

While we may never find ourselves in the same circumstance as Martha and Sharon, true intercessors should be on call 24/7 to say no to the enemy's tactics—his plots and plans—whenever needed to help annihilate his evil intentions.

In All Things

There are infinite problems and challenges facing women today. And there is a great need for women of faith to join the ranks and pray for victory in their personal lives, their families, their neighborhoods, their communities, their nation and their world. Where are the Deborahs and Esthers for these times?

The Deborahs are those who will get God's instructions and go to war against the enemy, confident that God goes before them to secure victory.

The Esthers are those who will intercede before the King on behalf of their people—those born for such a time as this who will pay the price to get a wicked decree reversed.

Satan has no legal power over us, although he continues to wreak havoc in the world. Our Savior, the seed of the woman (see Genesis 3:15), crushed his head and broke his power. Now it is up to us to exert the authority Jesus invested in us to take back the ground the enemy has stolen.

We are authorized by Jesus and empowered by the Holy Spirit to do battle. With our orders from God's Word, we Christian women must take our positions in God's army. Let's learn how to pray more effectively and how to fight in the spiritual realm until those we love are truly liberated and God's Kingdom is advanced in the earth.

"He who lives in you is greater (mightier) than he who is in the world" (1 John 4:4 AMPC). Therefore, we have nothing to fear. May the women who proclaim the good news become a great, invincible army!

Prayer

Lord, thank You for the lessons from the field we have learned from You, from other believers and from this book. May the Spirit of the Lord rest upon us—the "Spirit of wisdom and understanding, the Spirit of counsel and might, the Spirit of knowledge and of the reverential and obedient fear of the Lord" (Isaiah 11:2 AMPC). Give us the courage and tenacity of Deborah to see the enemy defeated and Your victory established in our lives and families and in our nation. We ask this in the precious name of Jesus, the captain of our salvation (see Hebrews 2:10 KJV). Amen.

Our friend James Goll has been an encourager to women in prayer ministry over the years and wrote a charge for modern-day Deborahs to become the warring women needed in today's world. We leave you with his challenge.

Now Is the Time for Godly Women to Arise!

by James Goll

I want to see a company of Deborahs arise in this hour across the spectrum of society. . . .

. . . As a male spiritual leader, I have something to say to you, mighty women of God! We cannot afford for you to be fearful "little women" in your own eyes. It is time for you to emerge! We need you!

. . . Come forth with internal security like Deborah of old and pick up your warrior's mantle for such a time as this. . . .

. . . It's time to arise and carry Deborah's heart and anointing! Yes, it must be a heart of purity mixed with the unshakable quality of courage.

. . . I say to you, "Come forth!" Come on now! Change society. Shift the courts. Bring revival and restoration to the land. . . .

Remember, you were chosen for such a time as this![5]

Epilogue

After the first edition of *A Woman's Guide to Spiritual Warfare* was released in 1991, we were inundated by letters from women whose lives had been deeply impacted by what they read. In the original book, we had included a story about a young man named Steve (which we have included again below), and we later received a letter from a woman who had read the story and provided us with a surprising piece of the story's puzzle.

The Original Story

Betty, who served on her church's counseling and deliverance team, was puzzled when her son developed a strange physical problem that did not respond to medical care or prayer.

Steve was in high school in the midseventies when he began having boils under both arms. After many prescriptions and weekly doctor visits, the physician lanced the boils, but they would not heal. Steve went to the doctor daily to get the wounds cauterized. Then he got a staph infection, requiring hospital stays and more treatment. After three years, doctors removed sweat glands from under both arms, but healing still eluded him.

One day while Betty was cleaning Steve's room, she found an old folded-up sheet of paper he had taken out of his wallet that morning. Printed on it was an Arabian curse that read, "Because you parked in my place, may the fleas of a thousand camels infest your armpits."

It seemed incredible. Could Steve's infirmity possibly be the result of a curse?

"I never suspected Steve could be the victim of a curse," Betty said. "But he had carried it in his wallet for three years, and for three years he'd had this problem. It was weird. He had so wanted to play football but couldn't because of the boils."

That afternoon when he got home, Steve and Betty destroyed the note and audibly declared in the name of Jesus that the curse was broken, along with any power that might be affecting his physical problem. Steve's healing came quickly, and never again was he bothered with irritation under his arms.

The Follow-Up Letter

A woman read a borrowed copy of *A Woman's Guide to Spiritual Warfare* a few months after its initial publication and was convicted when she read Steve's story. She recognized the description of her hometown in one of the other stories and remembered she had left such a note on a car in a campus parking lot while she was living there. This made her think she was involved in the mystery.

Writing to me (Quin), she said she never intended to put a curse on anyone. She had heard the silly statement on *The Tonight Show* and thought it was a harmless and witty way to express her irritation toward whoever had parked in her favorite spot on campus. To her greater shame, she said she never thought anything that seemed so innocent could have such powerful negative consequences.

She was horrified when she read the story because she believed she was the person who wrote the note Steve had been carrying around for three years. As soon as she read how it had caused him so much grief, she went to her knees in prayer, repented of her carelessness and asked God to forgive her. Though she was a Christian, she admitted she had been living a very lukewarm and selfish life.

The Holy Spirit impelled this woman to write to me, she said, so that I might ask Betty and Steve's forgiveness on her behalf for the years of suffering and expense they had endured because of her ignorance and sarcasm. She ended her letter with a request for me to tell them she prays for all the blessings of Deuteronomy 28:1–11 to be upon their household.

This is a mind-boggling case of how a seemingly innocent action can produce quite a negative outcome. As the story came full circle in a way only God could have orchestrated, all those involved in the experience received new insight into the seriousness of word curses.

Just as the woman ended her letter by declaring a blessing on Betty and Steve's family through words that carry spiritual power, we end this book in the hope that you will also learn to invoke blessings upon the lives of others.

The Warring Midwives

In October 1991, I (Ruthanne) was teaching on spiritual warfare at a prayer retreat in Beaumont, Texas, not long after the first version of this book went on the market. During that weekend, the Lord released the following word through me for the women attending the retreat:

I am making you warring midwives, to bring to birth in the spirit realm those whom the devouring lion seeks to destroy. These lambs in the jaws of the evil one are those I desire to use to help bring in the end-time harvest.

But you, My daughters, must travail in prayer and labor to wrench them from the grip of the enemy. Your tenacity in intercession and aggressive warfare will set these captives free. Understand that the enemy's grasp is strong because he knows the threat they will be to his kingdom if they escape his grasp.

Receive this commission, My daughters, to bring them to birth in the spirit realm. Then minister healing to their wounds, and love them with a mother's love and nurture. Then release them into their ministries in My harvest. Send them forth with your blessing and prayers, and know that you share in the great reward reserved for My warring midwives.

Over the years, I forgot I had given this word. But in June 2015, I came across a copy of it in an old file while preparing to teach a retreat in Dallas. As I pursued a study of the two Hebrew midwives in Exodus 1, I was struck by the reality that because two bold women defied Pharaoh's orders, Moses' life was spared. God ordered his steps as he was raised in the palace, then fled to the wilderness of Midian. But at last he became God's chosen deliverer to lead the Hebrews out of slavery.

Here is the midwives' courageous story:

Then Pharaoh, the king of Egypt, instructed the Hebrew midwives (their names were Shiphrah and Puah) to kill all Hebrew boys as soon as they were born, but to let the girls live. But the midwives feared God and didn't obey the king—they let the boys live too.

The king summoned them before him and demanded, "Why have you disobeyed my command and let the baby boys live?"

"Sir," they told him, "the Hebrew women have their babies so quickly that we can't get there in time! They are not slow like the Egyptian women!"

And God blessed the midwives because they were God-fearing women. So the people of Israel continued to multiply and to become a mighty nation.

Exodus 1:15–20 TLB

I was even more impressed when I looked up the meanings of the midwives' names. Shiphrah means "brightness; to glisten," and Puah means "to glitter; brilliancy." These warring midwives, though not named among the heroes of faith in Hebrews 11, certainly are shining heroines whose daring actions provided a mighty leader for the Hebrew people.

We stated in the first chapter of this book that a woman's place is in the war. That means we need to answer the call to become warring midwives for those living under a curse whom the enemy is holding in bondage. Those who seem to be bound by the heaviest chains imaginable may be the very ones with the greatest potential to lead others out of bondage.

We encourage you to ask the Holy Spirit to direct you to people for whom you are to stand in the gap—and then go to war against the enemy on their behalf, using the powerful weapons God provides. Receiving the reward and blessing of obedience will make your effort worth it all!

Appendix 1

Arsenal Scriptures for Spiritual Warfare

For Authority over the Enemy

Isaiah 44:25–26; 54:17; 55:11; 59:19
Jeremiah 1:12
Matthew 10:8; 12:28–29; 16:19
Mark 3:27; 6:7; 16:17
Luke 10:19
2 Corinthians 2:14
Ephesians 1:19–22; 4:8; 6:10–18
Colossians 2:15
Revelation 1:18

For Children

1 Kings 4:29
Psalm 127:3–5; 144:12
Isaiah 11:2; 43:5; 49:25; 54:13; 59:21
Jeremiah 29:11–14; 31:16–17
Daniel 1:9, 20
Ephesians 1:17; 6:4

Philippians 4:19
Colossians 1:9–12
James 1:2

For Dealing with an Abusive Husband

Leviticus 26:3–13
Deuteronomy 8:7–10
2 Chronicles 15:7
Psalm 31:20–21; 32:7; 91; 144:11; 145:18
Ezekiel 28:24–26

For Guidance

Psalm 34:19; 37:23–24; 123:1–2
Proverbs 3:5–6
Isaiah 30:21
2 Corinthians 5:7

For Healing

Exodus 15:26
Psalm 103:1–5
Proverbs 3:7–8; 4:20–22
Isaiah 53:5
Matthew 4:23; 9:28–29; 15:26–28
Mark 6:7, 12–13; 16:17–18
Luke 9:11
John 14:12–13
James 5:14–16
1 Peter 2:24
1 John 3:8
3 John 2

For the Nations

Joshua 1:3
Psalm 2:8; 68:32–35; 108:1–5
Jeremiah 1:10; 15:19–21; 51:21
Daniel 12:3
Micah 4:13

For a New Job

Deuteronomy 28:3–14; 31:8
Joshua 1:3, 5–9
2 Chronicles 15:7
Psalm 1:3

For Peace of Mind

Deuteronomy 33:27
Psalm 31:24
Isaiah 26:3
John 14:27
1 Corinthians 2:16
2 Corinthians 10:5
Ephesians 2:14–15
Philippians 4:7–9

For Protection

Deuteronomy 28:6–7
Psalm 5:11; 17:7–9; 91:1–7, 10
Proverbs 2:8
Isaiah 54:17

For Provision and Finances

Deuteronomy 8:18
1 Kings 17:2–4, 8–9
2 Chronicles 32:8
Proverbs 3:2; 10:3; 11:23, 25; 12:12;
    13:21–22, 25
Isaiah 54:5
Malachi 3:10–11
Matthew 6:25, 32
Luke 6:38

For Restoration and Security

Psalm 31:8; 32:7
Proverbs 10:30; 12:3, 21; 18:10
Joel 2:18–32

For Sleeplessness

Job 11:18–19
Psalm 4:8; 127:2
Proverbs 3:24
Matthew 11:28–30
Mark 4:37–39

For Strength and Declaration of Victory

1 Samuel 17:45
2 Samuel 22:33, 35, 40
2 Kings 6:16–17
Psalm 18:29; 68:28; 149:6–9
Song of Solomon 6:10
Isaiah 41:15; 50:7
Jeremiah 12:5; 23:29

For Those in Authority

Psalm 37:23
Proverbs 21:1
1 Timothy 2:1–2

For Wayward Family Members

Psalm 140:1–2, 4, 8
Isaiah 57:18–19; 59:1, 21
Jeremiah 33:26
2 Corinthians 4:3–4
2 Timothy 2:25–26

For Weariness and Depression

Psalm 28:7–9; 30:11–12; 55:18
Isaiah 40:28–31; 41:10; 43:2, 18–19;
   45:2–3

Why Pray

Ezekiel 22:30
1 Timothy 2:1–2
James 5:16

To Receive Jesus as Lord

John 3:7–8, 16; 6:37; 10:10; 14:6
Romans 3:23; 10:9–13
1 John 1:9

Appendix 2

Prayers and Declarations Based on Scripture

Against Counterattack

We have learned that after a ministry assignment or a season of spiritual warfare, it is important to secure the victory by breaking any counterattacks or backlash the enemy seeks to send against us, our families or our prayer partners. Here is a suggested prayer:

Thank You, Lord Jesus, that You have given us authority over the enemy by the power of Your shed blood. With that authority, I now address all God-hating spirits and declare that any curse or strategy of evil directed toward me, my family members, my prayer partners or the people to whom I have ministered is rendered null and void by the blood of Jesus Christ. I speak confusion to the ranks of the enemy, and I decree that no weapon formed against

me or God's purposes shall prosper but instead be con-
demned [see Isaiah 54:17]. *Thank You, Lord, that victory
is the heritage of Your people, and I lift up worship and
praise to Your holy name. Amen.*

Authority over the Enemy for Children

*In the name and under the authority of Jesus Christ, my
Lord, I bind all principalities and powers of evil in the
heavenly realm exerting influence over my child(ren),* [their
names], *and declare that the assignments against them are
cancelled by the blood of Jesus Christ. I bind and break
the spirits of witchcraft, mind control, occult activity, hard
rock music, lust, perversion, rebellion, rejection, suicide,
anger, hatred, unforgiveness, resentment, bitterness, pride,
deception, unbelief, fear, greed, addictions and* [others
the Lord reveals]. *I declare their power null and void in
the lives of my children—the blinders the enemy has put
on them must go, in Jesus' name.*

*My children will see the light of the Gospel of Christ;
they shall be taught of the Lord, and great will be their
peace* [see Isaiah 54:13]. *Thank You, Lord, that You guide*
[child's name] *in the paths of righteousness for Your
name's sake and that goodness and mercy will follow him/
her all the days of his/her life* [see Psalm 23:3, 6]. *I release
them to be all that God created them to be!*

Hedge of Protection

*Strengthen the hedge of protection around me, my family
and my possessions this day, Lord. Thank You for being
my shield and protector.*

216

Guidance

*O Lord, direct my steps and give me knowledge, wisdom
and understanding beyond my experience for decisions
facing me. May the Holy Spirit guide me into all truth
and give me Your peace.*

Help in a Hurry

*All-powerful God, I ask in the name of Jesus that You
send angelic forces to sabotage the enemy's strategic plans
and attacks against me and/or* [name of person] *and/or*
[name of situation]. *Thank You, dear Lord.*

Opposing Satanic Harassment

*In the name and authority of Jesus Christ of Nazareth, I
oppose any satanic tactics or strategies that are designed
to hinder or delay God's plans and purposes from mani-
festing in their correct time and season in my family's life*
[see Daniel 7:25]. *Lord, as for me, I seek You! I place my
cause before You, the God who does great and unsearch-
able things, wonders without number. God, frustrate the
plotting of the shrewd and evil, so that their hands cannot attain success, so that the helpless has hope. May the
unrighteous shut their mouths. Hide me from the scourge
of the tongue* [see Job 5:8–9, 12, 16, 21 NASB]. *Further-
more, no weapon formed against me/us shall prosper, and
every tongue that accuses me/us in judgment I/we will
condemn, because this is the heritage of the servants of
the Lord, and their vindication is from God* [see Isaiah
54:17 NASB].

Breaking Curses

I declare that any curse that has ever been spoken against me and/or my family—any negative, evil word that has ever come against us—is broken right now, in the name and authority of Jesus Christ of Nazareth. We are covered by the blood of Jesus Christ, and the curses of the enemy are broken [see Galatians 3:13].

Declaration of Victory

I declare that everything I put my hands to do is going to succeed and prosper. When the enemy shall come in, like a flood, God's Spirit lifts up a standard against him [see Isaiah 59:16–19]. *"With God we will gain the victory, and he will trample down our enemies"* [Psalm 60:12].

Day-to-Day Family Life

Lord, I ask for You to bestow upon me and my family Your presence, provision and protection, and for Your precious promises to be fulfilled in our lives. I thank You that we are victors, not victims. You are fighting our battles for us. We have the favor of God.

Family with Division

We cry out for mercy today for our family, Lord. When the enemy comes in to divide, confuse and bring disunity, anger or hurt, Father God, intervene and be our healer and deliverer. Strengthen and restore our family. In Jesus' name, Amen.

Favor

"Surely, LORD, you bless the righteous; you surround them with your favor as with a shield" [Psalm 5:12]. I thank You for doing this for me and my family.

Finances

Lord, I war for the enemy to release finances and all resources that You want me to have for completing the great work You have given me to accomplish here on earth. I call in the resources necessary for me to do God's will to come without delay. Father, I thank You in advance for the wisdom and discernment I need to accomplish that task and to use wisely the resources You provide.

Financial Lack

When financial setbacks attempt to lure us into fear, Lord, may we stand firm on Your promises. I bind every tactic of the enemy. Get off, get out, get away from our family's finances. You will not steal nor withhold from us what is rightfully ours through Christ. We declare that all our needs are met according to God's glorious riches in Christ Jesus. He has not given us a spirit of fear but of power, love and a sound mind [see Philippians 4:19 and 2 Timothy 1:7].

Elections

Father, we pray that moral, God-fearing men and women be elected and supported in local, state and national elections. We pray for You to reveal Your choices and for

You to expose corruption, immorality, bribery, hidden agendas and special interests. May any unrighteousness that needs uncovering be brought to light and exposed. Let Christians be responsible voters and use the Bible as their plumb line.

Marriages

Lord, help our nation to return the state of marriage to a place of honor and to establish this sacred institution in Your divine order. For marriages that are strained, bring hope, healing and restoration. Let Your Holy Spirit direct those couples who are facing critical decisions and seeking godly wisdom. Guard our families from strife and division, and invade these homes with Your presence, joy and peace.

Nation

Father, as we stand in the gap for our nation, cities and families, we declare that the power of the blood of Jesus breaks every chain of bondage. We seek Your face, Lord, and repent of our sins—we are truly sorry for the way we have broken Your laws and disobeyed You. Thank You for forgiving us.

Please heal our land. We declare that no weapon formed against our nation shall prosper. Every tongue that would rise up against us in judgment will be exposed and cast down. We pray for the manifold wisdom of God to rest upon all who are in authority over our country. May truth and discernment guide every decision they make in their public and private lives. May any unrighteous officials currently in office be replaced by those who will serve with integrity. We cry for justice and mercy, truth and righteousness to be established [see Proverbs 21:1–2; Isaiah 54:17; Romans 8:26–31; 16:20; Ephesians 3:10; 6:10–20; 1 Timothy 2:1–4].

Guard our nation, dear Lord—our borders, military bases, educational facilities, public buildings, stadiums, ports, ship channels, bridges, the postal system, all transportation systems (airlines, trains, buses, autos), water conduits, electrical and nuclear energy plants, gas/oil distribution centers, hospital and medical facilities, space center and research facilities, homes and law enforcement services [add others as the Lord shows you].

False Religion

Father, shield and protect our nation from occultism, New Age deception, false religions and secret societies. Reverse the trends of humanism and socialism in our culture. May the Body of Christ be salt and light by speaking the truth in love to those who are seeking to know the truth in the midst of today's confused, chaotic world. We pray that the knowledge of the glory of the Lord will cover our nation as the waters cover the sea [see Matthew 5:13–16; Habakkuk 2:14].

Praise

We enter Your gates with thanksgiving and Your courts with praise. Lord, we give thanks to You and praise Your name. For You, Lord, are good, and Your love endures forever; Your faithfulness continues through all generations. You are enthroned over our nation through the praises of Your people. Praise and glory and wisdom and thanks and honor and power and strength be to our God forever and ever [see Psalm 100:4–5; 22:3; Revelation 7:12]. *Amen.*

Promises

Thank You, Lord, for Your promise that You will fulfill Your purpose for me and my family and will not abandon the works of Your hands [see Psalm 138:8].

Salvation for Those Who Do Not Know Jesus

God, it is not Your will that any should perish but that all would come to repentance [see 2 Peter 3:9]. *Therefore, I pray, God, grant* [name of person] *repentance leading to the knowledge of the truth and grant that he/she may come to his/her senses and escape from the snare of the devil, having been held captive by him to do his will* [see 2 Timothy 2:25–26].

Times of Trouble

With the psalmist, we cry out, "Then they cried to the Lord *in their trouble. . . . He brought them out of darkness, the utter darkness, and broke away their chains"* [Psalm 107:13–14]. *We stand on Your Word and ask You to do this for us as we, Your children, cry out in trouble and distress. Please, Lord, rescue us. Break down gates of bronze, and cut through bars of iron. Save us. You stilled the storm and guided Your people to their desired haven, so we thank You in advance that You will do it for us. With the psalmist, we, too, give thanks to You, Lord, for Your unfailing love and blessings and for lifting us from affliction* [see Psalm 107:15, 41]. [You can personalize this prayer with the names of those for whom you are praying.]

Terrorism

Lord, let any terrorist schemes against our nation and cities be exposed and stopped—absolutely thwarted—before they can be carried out. Help those who guard our borders, ports and airways who are charged with keeping the nation safe to do their job with diligence and watchfulness. Draw their attention to anything amiss that needs to be investigated, and keep them from harm.

Youth

Give the youth of our nation hearts to follow You, Lord— to live godly lives and to fulfill Your purposes for them. Turn the hearts of fathers to their children and the hearts of children to their fathers in a loving way. Forgive us where we have failed. Raise up a generation of young people who will do great exploits for You [see Malachi 4:6; Daniel 11:32].

A Suggested Prayer Strategy

I (Quin) have pictures pinned to a corkboard that is hanging on the wall above my computer. A family montage, you may think. Not quite. This select sea of faces are people for whom I pray regularly. My "prayer board" has been around for more than three decades. Photos are updated yearly; boards are replaced as needed.

Twenty-eight faces are those of friends. The rest are immediate and extended family, photographed in groups—such as my 94-year-old aunt, surrounded by her six children. Photos on my board include pastors, businesspeople, homemakers, moms, singles, college students, retirees and widows. A few have health issues or are undergoing dialysis or chemotherapy. Some travel to foreign countries regularly on Kingdom business. One 83-year-old seldom travels farther than the downtown church but spends time each day in her prayer chair, interceding for those in her sphere of influence.

When I pray for them, I first pray that they will experience God's:

- Presence (Psalm 16:11; 31:20; 41:12; 51:10–12)
- Protection (Psalm 5:11; 72:12–14; 91:14–16; 121:7–8)
- Provision (Joshua 2:8–9; Psalm 106:4–5; 128:1–2; Philippians 4:19)
- Peace (Psalm 4:8; 29:11; 122:7–9; 147:14)
- Precious promises to be fulfilled (2 Corinthians 1:20; 2:14; 2 Peter 1:4)

Next, I pray specifically for various situations in their lives I may know about. These prayers may include for them to:

- Have discernment and wisdom and not be deceived in decisions facing them
- Make wise choices financially and morally
- Find favor in the marketplace
- Cast their cares, worries and anxieties on the Lord, trusting Him
- Have the right people come into their life at the right time
- Have a positive influence as they use their talents and skills to help others
- Experience God's healing and comforting touch

Many of these individuals also intercede for me, but some do not yet have a relationship with Christ. For them, I pray in faith based on these Scriptures: "The Lord is not slow in keeping his promise, as some understand slowness. He is patient with you, not wanting anyone to perish, but everyone to come to repentance" (2 Peter 3:9), and "Jesus answered, 'I am the way and the truth and the life. No man comes to the Father except through me'" (see John 14:6).

Have you considered how you can affect the people in your field of influence—simply by praying for them? Making a prayer board does not take much time or energy. Collect pictures sent at Christmastime, or request small headshots of those for whom you plan to pray specifically. Contact them periodically to see if they have new requests.

Email, texts and phone calls are fast ways for prayer partners to relay requests. I often record the spoken needs in a private prayer journal, then go back and write down God's answers when they happen. I have stacks of notes from my prayer-board friends that have made my prayer efforts joyous.

Why not try it yourself? You will be in for a rewarding adventure!

Notes

Chapter 1: But I Never Wanted to Be in a Battle!

1. Barna Group, "Most American Christians Do Not Believe That Satan or the Holy Spirit Exist," April 13, 2009, https://www.barna.org/barna-update/faith-spirituality/260-most-american-christians-do-not-believe-that-satan-or-the-holy-spirit-exis#.V1hEupMrLeQ (accessed June 8, 2016).

2. C. S. Lewis, *The Screwtape Letters* (New York: Macmillan, 1961), 3.

3. Herbert Lockyer, *All the Women of the Bible* (Grand Rapids, Mich.: Zondervan Books, 1988), 41.

4. This story is adapted from Quin Sherrer and Ruthanne Garlock, *Lord, I Need Your Healing Power* (Lake Mary, Fla.: Charisma House, 2006), 3–4.

Chapter 2: Who Is the Enemy, and What Does He Want from Me?

1. R. Arthur Mathews, *Born for Battle: 31 Studies on Spiritual Warfare* (Robesonia, Pa.: OMF Books, 2008), 28.

2. Dean Sherman, *Spiritual Warfare for Every Christian: How to Live in Victory and Retake the Land* (Seattle: YWAM Publishing, 1990), 90.

3. Ibid., 92.

4. McCandlish Phillips, *The Bible, the Supernatural, and the Jews* (New York: World Publishing, 1970), 73.

5. Edith Schaeffer, *A Way of Seeing* (Old Tappan, N.J.: Revell, 1977), 110.

6. William Gurnall, *The Christian in Complete Armour*, vol. 1, abridged by Ruthanne Garlock et al. (Carlisle, Pa.: Banner of Truth Trust, 1986), 54.

7. Richard D. Dobbins, "Caring for the Casualties," *Charisma*, September 1990, 96.

Chapter 3: What Our Spiritual Wardrobe Should Look Like

1. Gurnall, *Christian in Complete Armour*, vol. 1, 66, 68, 69.

2. William Gurnall, *The Christian in Complete Armour*, vol. 2, abridged by Ruthanne Garlock et al. (Carlisle, Pa.: Banner of Truth Trust, 1986), 22–23.

3. W. E. Vine, *Vine's Expository Dictionary of Old and New Testament Words*, vol. 3 (Old Tappan, N.J.: Fleming H. Revell, 1981), 298–99.

4. Gurnall, *Christian in Complete Armour*, vol. 2, 160.

5. Rick Renner, *Sparkling Gems from the Greek: 365 Greek Word Studies for Every Day of the Year to Sharpen Your Understanding of God's Word* (Tulsa, Okla.: Teach All Nations, 2003), 158.

6. Ibid., 158–159.

7. William Gurnall, *The Christian in Complete Armour*, vol. 3, abridged by Ruthanne Garlock et al. (Carlisle, Pa.: Banner of Truth Trust, 1986), 27–28, 30–31.

8. Sherman, *Spiritual Warfare for Every Christian*, 45.

9. W. E. Vine, *Vine's Expository Dictionary of Old and New Testament Words*, vol. 3 (Old Tappan, N.J.: Fleming H. Revell, 1981), 230.

10. Mathews, *Born for Battle*, 16.

11. Ibid., 20.

12. Gurnall, *Christian in Complete Armour*, vol. 3, 164.

Chapter 4: How Strong Can a Woman Be?

1. Associated Press, "Study: Moms Credited Most in Instilling Faith," *Florida Daily News*, February 10, 1990.

2. John Dawson, *Taking Our Cities for God: How to Break Spiritual Strongholds*, rev. ed. (Lake Mary, Fla.: Charisma House, 2001), 10–11.

3. Judson Cornwall, *Praying the Scriptures: Using God's Words to Effect Change in All of Life's Situations*, 3rd ed. (Lake Mary, Fla.: Charisma House, 2008), 201–202.

Chapter 5: The Disciplines of the Spirit-Empowered Woman

1. Finis Jennings Dake, *Dake's Annotated Reference Bible* (Lawrenceville, Ga.: Dake Bible Sales, 1963), 629. Other references given by Dake include Psalm 35:13; 69:10; 2 Samuel 12:16–23; Ezra 8:21; Matthew 4:1–11; 6:16–18; 9:15; Luke 5:33; Acts 9:7–9; 13:1–5; 1 Corinthians 7:5.

2. Arthur Wallis, *God's Chosen Fast: A Spiritual and Practical Guide to Fasting* (Fort Washington, Pa.: Christian Literature Crusade, 1968), 41–42, 86.

3. Partially excerpted from Quin Sherrer, *A Mother's Guide to Praying for Your Children* (Minneapolis: Chosen, 2011, 2014), 99–100; and further supported by recent interviews.

Chapter 6: Our Weapons and Strategy

1. Paul E. Billheimer, *Destined to Overcome* (Minneapolis: Bethany House, 2006), 41, 43.

2. Sherman, *Spiritual Warfare for Every Christian*, 123.

3. H. A. Maxwell Whyte, *The Power of the Blood*, rev. ed. (New Kensington, Pa.: Whitaker House, 2005), 63.

4. Ibid., 120.

5. Mathews, *Born for Battle*, 66.

6. Ibid., 124.

7. Adapted from Sherrer and Garlock, *Lord, I Need Your Healing Power*, 133–134.

Chapter 7: An Open Door to the Enemy

1. *The E. W. Bullinger Companion Bible* (Grand Rapids, Mich.: Zondervan, 1964), appendix 44, iv.

2. Other references concerning the sins of the fathers are Deuteronomy 29:24–28; 2 Chronicles 7:19–22; 34:23–25; Ezra 9:4, 13–15; Nehemiah 9:1–3; Isaiah 65:6–7; Jeremiah 14:20–22; 16:10–13.

3. Burton Stokes and Lynn Lucas, *No Longer a Victim: Answers for the Pain Inside* (Shippensburg, Pa.: Destiny Image, 1988), 25.

4. Derek Prince, *Blessing or Curse: You Can Choose*, 3rd ed. (Grand Rapids, Mich.: Chosen Books, 2006), 22, 161.

5. Phillips, *The Bible, the Supernatural, and the Jews*, 75–77.

6. Herbert Lockyer Sr., gen. ed., *Nelson's Illustrated Bible Dictionary: An Authoritative One-Volume Reference Work on the Bible, with Full-Color Illustrations* (Nashville: Thomas Nelson, 1986), 501.

7. Ed Murphy, "We Are at War," in *Wrestling with Dark Angels: Toward a Deeper Understanding of the Supernatural Forces in Spiritual Warfare*, eds. C. Peter Wagner and F. Douglas Pennoyer, rev. ed. (Eugene, Ore.: Wipf and Stock, 1990), 60.

8. Ibid., 68, 70–71.

9. This story is adapted from Quin Sherrer and Ruthanne Garlock, *Lord, I Need to Pray with Power* (Lake Mary, Fla.: Charisma House, 2009), 177.

10. Dutch Sheets, *Intercessory Prayer: How God Can Use Your Prayers to Move Heaven and Earth*, rev. ed. (Minneapolis: Bethany House, 1996, 2016), 232–33.

Chapter 8: Breaking Bondages

1. Archibald D. Hart, *Healing Life's Hidden Addictions: Overcoming the Closet Compulsions That Waste Your Time and Control Your Life* (Ann Arbor, Mich.: Servant Publications, 1990), 238.

2. We recommend Jan Frank's book, *A Door of Hope: Recognizing and Resolving the Pains of Your Past*, rev. ed. (Nashville: Thomas Nelson, 1995), which provides steps toward recovery from abuse, based on her experience as a victim of incest, and provides answers to common questions asked by abuse victims and those who seek to help them.

3. Statistics regarding the aftereffects of abortion, as well as helpful resources for postabortion women, are available at www.afterabortion.org, sponsored by the Elliot Institute, P.O. Box 7348, Springfield, IL 62791–7348.

4. Excerpted from Anonymous, "One Woman's Walk through an Abortion Nightmare," *Charisma* (October 1990), 96–108. Used by permission of the author.

Chapter 9: Fight for Your Children

1. Mel Gabler, *Have You Read Your Child's School Textbooks?* (Longview, Tex.: Educational Research Analysts, now out of print). Mel Gabler's Educational Research Analysts website is located at www.textbookreviews.org.

2. David Barton, "Revisionism: How to Identify It in Your Children's Textbooks," WallBuilders.com, January 2005, http://www.wallbuilders.com/libiss uesarticles.asp?id=112.

3. Gateways to Better Education provides helpful articles and information on this issue, available at www.gtbe.org/news.

4. Gregory R. Reid, *Trojan Church: The New Age Corruption of the Evangelical Faith* (Longwood, Fla.: Xulon Press, 2008), 33, 48. Learn more about Dr. Reid and YouthFire at www.gregoryreid.com.

5. Greg Reid, *Teen Satanism: Redeeming the Devil's Children* (Columbus, Ga.: Quill Publications, 1990), 9.

6. Adapted from Quin Sherrer and Ruthanne Garlock, *Lord, Help Me Break This Habit: You Can Be Free from Doing the Things You Hate* (Grand Rapids, Mich.: Chosen, 2009), 149–50.

7. Barna Group, "Survey Describes the Ups and Downs of Tween Life," September 30, 2006, https://www.barna.org/barna-update/family-kids/146-survey -describes-the-ups-and-downs-of-tween-life#.V403OpMrLeQ.

8. Quin Sherrer and Ruthanne Garlock, *Praying Prodigals Home: Taking Back What the Enemy Has Stolen* (Minneapolis: Chosen, 2000, 2014), 28.

9. Adapted from Sherrer and Garlock, *Lord, I Need to Pray with Power*, 58–59.

Chapter 10: Fight for Your Marriage

1. *Time*, "What Youth Think," special issue, *Women: The Road Ahead*, Fall 1990, 14.

2. James Dobson, *Love Must Be Tough: New Hope for Families in Crisis* (Waco, Tex.: Word Books, 1996), 134.

3. Ibid., 134–135.

4. Ibid., 77.

5. Archibald D. Hart, *Helping Children Survive Divorce: What to Expect; How to Help*, rev. ed. (Nashville: Thomas Nelson, 1996), 27.

6. Bob Gass, "Tough Love," *The Word for You Today*, Third Quarter 2009, 34.

7. Hart, *Helping Children Survive Divorce*, 47–62.

8. Judy Reamer, *Feelings Women Rarely Share* (Springdale, Pa: Whitaker House, 1987), 89, 92, 145.

Chapter 11: Healing and Spiritual Warfare

1. Reginald Cherry, MD, *Healing Prayer: God's Divine Intervention in Medicine, Faith and Prayer* (Nashville: Thomas Nelson, 1999), 116–117.

2. Arlene Strackbein, "Battle of the Mind," *Mighty Warrior* newsletter, Summer 1989, 6–7, 9.

3. Stanley Howard Frodsham, *Smith Wigglesworth: Apostle of Faith* (Springfield, Mo.: Gospel Publishing House, 2002), 111.

4. James W. Goll, *The Prophetic Intercessor: Releasing God's Purposes to Change Lives and Influence Nations*, rev. ed. (Grand Rapids, Mich.: Chosen, 2007). Adapted from pages 36-43 and from personal interviews.

Chapter 12: Are You under Attack?

1. Dean Sherman (lecture, Christ for the Nations Institute, Dallas, Fall 1990).

2. This story is adapted from Quin Sherrer and Ruthanne Garlock, *Prayer Partnerships: Experiencing the Power of Agreement* (Ann Arbor, Mich.: Servant Publications, 2001), 121–22.

Chapter 13: Lessons from the Field

1. Adapted from Sherrer and Garlock, *Lord, I Need to Pray with Power*, 7.

2. Dawson, *Taking Our Cities for God*, 148.

3. Anne J. Townsend, *Prayer without Pretending* (Chicago: Moody, 1973), 45–46.

4. Adapted from Martha Lucia, *Rules of Engagement*, vol. 2 (Santa Rosa Beach, Fla.: Christian International Publishing, 2009) 40–41, plus personal interviews. Used with permission.

5. James W. Goll, "Now Is the Time for Godly Women to Arise!," The Elijah List, July 7, 2015, http://www.elijahlist.com/words/display_word.html?ID=14911. Used with permission. Learn more about James Goll's ministry at www.james goll.com.

Recommended Reading

Alves, Elizabeth. *Becoming a Prayer Warrior: A Guide to Effective and Powerful Prayer.* Minneapolis: Chosen, 2016.

Anderson, Neil T. *The Bondage Breaker.* 2nd ed. Eugene, Ore.: Harvest House, 2000.

———. *Victory Over the Darkness.* 2nd ed. Minneapolis: Bethany House, 2013, 2014.

Billheimer, Paul E. *Destined to Overcome.* Minneapolis: Bethany House, 2006.

Cornwall, Judson. *Praying the Scriptures: Using God's Words to Effect Change in All of Life's Situations.* 3rd ed. Lake Mary, Fla.: Charisma House, 2008.

Dawson, John. *Taking Our Cities for God: How to Break Spiritual Strongholds.* Rev. ed. Lake Mary, Fla.: Charisma House, 2001.

Dobson, James. *Love Must Be Tough: New Hope for Families in Crisis.* Carol Stream, Ill.: Tyndale, 2007.

Frank, Jan. *A Door of Hope: Recognizing and Resolving the Pains of Your Past.* Rev. ed. Nashville: Thomas Nelson, 1995.

Garlock, H. B., with Ruthanne Garlock. *Before We Kill and Eat You: Tales of Faith in the Face of Certain Death.* 4th ed. Broken Arrow, Okla.: Timothy Publishing Services, 2014.

Goll, James W. *The Lost Art of Intercession: Restoring the Power and Passion of the Watch of the Lord.* Shippensburg, Pa.: Destiny Image, 1997.

———. *The Prophetic Intercessor: Releasing God's Purposes to Change Lives and Influence Nations.* Rev. ed. Grand Rapids, Mich.: Chosen, 2007.

Gurnall, William. *The Christian in Complete Armour*. Abridged by Ruthanne Garlock et. al. 3 vols. Carlisle, Pa.: Banner of Truth Trust, 1986, 1988, 1989.

Hamon, Jane. *The Deborah Company: Becoming a Woman Who Makes a Difference*. Shippensburg, Pa.: Destiny Image, 2007.

Hart, Archibald D. *Healing Life's Hidden Addictions: Overcoming the Closet Compulsions That Waste Your Time and Control Your Life*. Ann Arbor, Mich.: Servant Publications, 1990.

Jacobs, Cindy. *Possessing the Gates of the Enemy: A Training Manual for Militant Intercession*. 3rd ed. Grand Rapids, Mich.: Chosen, 2009.

———. *The Reformation Manifesto: Your Part in God's Plan to Change Nations Today*. Minneapolis: Bethany House, 2008.

Lewis, C. S. *The Screwtape Letters*. New York: HarperOne, 2001.

Mathews, R. Arthur. *Born for Battle: 31 Studies on Spiritual Warfare*. Robesonia, Pa.: OMF Books, 2008.

Michaelson, Johanna. *Like Lambs to the Slaughter: Your Child and the Occult*. Eugene, Ore.: Harvest House, 1989.

Phillips, McCandlish. *The Bible, the Supernatural, and the Jews*. New York: World Publishing, 1970.

Pierce, Chuck D., and Rebecca Wagner Sytsema. *Protecting Your Home from Spiritual Darkness*. Rev. ed. Minneapolis: Chosen, 2004, 2014.

Prince, Derek. *Blessing or Curse: You Can Choose*. 3rd ed. Grand Rapids, Mich.: Chosen, 2006.

Reamer, Judy. *Feelings Women Rarely Share*. Rev. ed. Springdale, Pa.: Whitaker House, 2003.

Reid, Greg. *Teen Satanism: Redeeming the Devil's Children*. Columbus, Ga.: Quill Publications, 1990. Available from YouthFire, P.O. Box 370006, El Paso, TX 79937.

Schaeffer, Edith. *A Way of Seeing*. Old Tappan, N.J.: Revell, 1977.

Sheets, Dutch. *An Appeal to Heaven*. Colorado Springs: Dutch Sheets Ministries, 2015.

———. *Authority in Prayer: Praying with Power and Purpose*. Minneapolis: Bethany House, 2006.

———. *Intercessory Prayer: How God Can Use Your Prayers to Move Heaven and Earth*. Rev. ed. Minneapolis: Bethany House, 1996, 2016.

———. *Watchman Prayer: Keeping the Enemy Out While Protecting Your Family, Home, and Community.* Rev. ed. Minneapolis: Bethany House, 2008, 2014.

Sherman, Dean. *Spiritual Warfare for Every Christian: How to Live in Victory and Retake the Land.* Seattle: YWAM Publishing, 1990.

Sherrer, Quin. *A Mother's Guide to Praying for Your Children.* Minneapolis: Chosen, 2011, 2014.

———. *Hope for a Widow's Heart: Encouraging Reflections for Your Journey.* Franklin, Tenn.: Authentic Publishers, 2013.

Sherrer, Quin, and Ruthanne Garlock. *The Beginner's Guide to Receiving the Holy Spirit.* Minneapolis: Chosen, 2011, 2015.

———. *Grandma, I Need Your Prayers: Blessing Your Grandchildren through the Power of Prayer.* Grand Rapids, Mich.: Zondervan, 2002.

———. *Lord, Help Me Break This Habit: You Can Be Free from Doing the Things You Hate.* Grand Rapids, Mich.: Chosen, 2009.

———. *Lord, I Need to Pray with Power.* Lake Mary, Fla.: Charisma House, 2009.

———. *Lord, I Need Your Healing Power.* Lake Mary, Fla.: Charisma House, 2006.

———. *Praying Prodigals Home: Taking Back What the Enemy Has Stolen.* Minneapolis: Chosen, 2000, 2014.

———. *The Spiritual Warrior's Prayer Guide.* 2nd ed. Minneapolis: Chosen, 2010, 2014.

Smith, Alice. *Delivering the Captives: Understanding the Strongman—and How to Defeat Him.* Minneapolis: Bethany House, 2006.

Wagner, C. Peter. *Praying with Power: How to Pray Effectively and Hear Clearly from God.* Shippensburg, Pa.: Destiny Image, 2008.

Wagner, C. Peter, and F. Douglas Pennoyer, eds. *Wrestling with Dark Angels: Toward a Deeper Understanding of the Supernatural Forces in Spiritual Warfare.* Rev. ed. Eugene, Ore.: Wipf and Stock, 1990.

Wallis, Arthur. *God's Chosen Fast: A Spiritual and Practical Guide to Fasting.* Fort Washington, Pa.: Christian Literature Crusade, 1968.

White, Thomas B. *The Believer's Guide to Spiritual Warfare.* 2nd ed. Minneapolis: Chosen, 2011, 2014.

Whyte, H. A. Maxwell. *The Power of the Blood.* New Kensington, Pa.: Whitaker House, 1973, 2005.

About the Authors

Quin Sherrer has written or co-authored 29 books, exceeding a million copies, including the bestsellers *The Spiritual Warrior's Prayer Guide, How to Pray for Your Children* and *Miracles Happen When You Pray*. Her book *Hope for a Widow's Heart* addresses all aspects of this difficult journey for women.

She has spoken to audiences in 48 states and 12 nations, encouraging them in their daily and sometimes challenging walks of faith. As a guest on more than 350 radio and television programs—including *The 700 Club, 100 Huntley Street* and various shows on the Daystar Television Network and the Trinity Broadcasting Network—she has addressed topics of prayer, hospitality, miracles, personal renewal and widowhood.

Quin holds a B.S. degree in journalism from Florida State University and currently lives in northern Florida. She spent her early career writing for newspapers and magazines in the Cape Kennedy, Florida, area, where her late husband, LeRoy, was a NASA engineer. A winner of *Guideposts* magazine's writing contest, she also was named Writer of the Year at the Florida Writers In Touch Conference. For a number of years she served in leadership roles for Aglow International, and she continues to speak at their retreats and at church seminars.

Quin has three children and six grandchildren. You can contact her through her website at www.quinsherrer.com.

Ruthanne Garlock is a Bible teacher and author with a varied background in international ministry to 35 nations. She has co-authored (with Quin Sherrer) nineteen books on prayer and related subjects. Their book *God Be with Us: A Daily Guide to Praying for Our Nation* was nominated for the 2002 Gold Medallion Award in the devotional category by the Evangelical Christian Publishers Association. Ruthanne was also the ghostwriter for two missions biographies, including *Before We Kill and Eat You: Tales of Faith in the Face of Certain Death*, about her father-in-law's pioneer missions work in Liberia in the 1920s.

For four years, Ruthanne and her husband, John, served with Continental Theological Seminary in Brussels, Belgium, and then for 23 years lived in Dallas, Texas, where John was an instructor at Christ for the Nations Institute and Ruthanne worked as a freelance writer and teacher. Since John's death in 2003, she continues to travel and teach on prayer and spiritual warfare at seminars, churches and women's groups.

Ruthanne holds a degree in Bible and religious education from Central Bible College, Springfield, Missouri, and is ordained with World Ministry Fellowship, Plano, Texas. Now living in the Texas Hill Country near San Antonio, she has three children and four grandchildren. You can contact her at the following:

Ruthanne Garlock
P.O. Box 53
Bulverde, TX 78163
www.garlockministries.org

More from the Authors

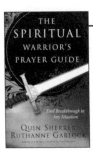

God's Word is the strongest weapon in your spiritual arsenal. When you use the Bible in intercession and spiritual warfare, you can bind the power of the evil one and declare God's victory in your own life and the lives of others. Discover how to apply biblical promises to every area of life, from illness to financial trouble to depression—and more!

The Spiritual Warrior's Prayer Guide by Quin Sherrer and Ruthanne Garlock

Do you know how to pray effectively and powerfully for your children? This step-by-step guide to praying for your sons and daughters will show you how to pray for your children's specific needs and circumstances, including prayers for protection against spiritual attack, prayers for your children's teachers and friends and more.

A Mother's Guide to Praying for Your Children by Quin Sherrer

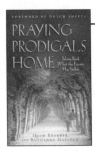

Quin Sherrer and Ruthanne Garlock have both endured the pain of waiting for the return of prodigal children. Here, they help you place your situation in God's hands—and reveal how to actively battle for your child as you wait expectantly for Him to move. Learn how to pray your prodigal home, and how the experience can draw you into the arms of your heavenly Father.

Praying Prodigals Home by Quin Sherrer and Ruthanne Garlock

✓Chosen

Stay up to date on your favorite books and authors with our free e-newsletters. Sign up today at chosenbooks.com.

Find us on Facebook. facebook.com/chosenbooks

Follow us on Twitter. @Chosen_Books